W9-CEU-607

Loving People Who Are Hard to Love

Loving People Who Are Hard to Love

Transforming Your World by
Learning to Love Unconditionally

JOYCE MEYER

NEW YORK • NASHVILLE

FaithWords
Hachette Book Group
1290 Avenue of the Americas, New York, NY 10104
faithwords.com
twitter.com/faithwords

First Edition: September 2022

FaithWords is a division of Hachette Book Group, Inc.
The FaithWords name and logo are trademarks of Hachette Book Group, Inc.

The publisher is not responsible for websites (or their content)
that are not owned by the publisher.

The Hachette Speakers Bureau provides a wide range of authors for speaking events. To find out more, go to www.hachettespeakersbureau.com or call (866) 376-6591.

The author would like to thank Beth Clark for her excellent editorial work on this project.

Library of Congress Cataloging-in-Publication Data
Names: Meyer, Joyce, author.
Title: Loving people who are hard to love : transforming your world by learning to love unconditionally / Joyce Meyer.
Description: First edition. | New York, NY : FaithWords, 2022.
Identifiers: LCCN 2022019438 | ISBN 9781546016090 (hardcover) | ISBN 9781546000341 | ISBN 9781546000648 | ISBN 9781546001768 (ebook)
Subjects: LCSH: Interpersonal relations—Religious aspects—Christianity. | Love—Religious aspects—Christianity.
Classification: LCC BV4597.52 .M49 2022 | DDC 248.4—dc23/eng/20220617
LC record available at https://lccn.loc.gov/2022019438

ISBNs: 978-1-5460-1609-0 (hardcover), 978-1-5460-0064-8 (large type), 978-1-5460-0176-8 (ebook)

Printed in the United States of America

LSC-H

Printing 1, 2022

CONTENTS

I don't think it is a secret that our world today is facing huge problems. There is more anger, hatred, violence, lack of peace, lack of real love, and turmoil than I have ever seen. I am not ancient, but I am seventy-eight years old, as of the writing of this book, so I've lived through a few decades. Of course, in every decade there are problems, but not as many or perhaps even as serious as the ones we face today.

Martin Luther King Jr. said, "We must learn to live together as brothers or perish together as fools." I believe this observation applies today perhaps even more than when he said it in 1964. When he made this statement, he was speaking about racial issues, but I believe it is perfect for the challenges we face today, which include not only racial issues but also mass shootings, random acts of violence, hate crimes, abortion, gender confusion, and a shocking increase in reports of mental illness and suicide, especially among young people.

What is the answer to the challenges we deal with in the world right now? It's certainly not that someone else needs to do something to change the situations we face. Each of us must do what needs to be done to change what we can change. We must learn to live in peace and walk in love. And we absolutely must learn to love people who are hard to love, which includes most of us, because we can all be difficult for others to love, at least at times. Love is much more than a feeling; it is how we treat people.

When I began to think about writing this book on loving people who are hard to love, I also thought about people who are easy to love. I concluded that I may know two people who are so easy to love that I do not have to make any effort to love them. But if I knew these people better, I might have to exclude them too.

Unless we become really good at not being easily offended and extending forgiveness to those who hurt us, I don't think there is any hope for peace and unity in the world. If you'd like to know what God's Word says about this, I have included in the appendix to this book a list of Scripture references that will help you forgive and find freedom from offense.

Satan has a plan for humanity, and sadly, at this point in history, many people seem to be playing along with it. His plan is to divide and conquer, because he knows that if people don't unite, he can defeat us. According to Ephesians 6:12, we are in a spiritual war, not a natural one. The only way we can win this battle is to truly love one another, because I believe the Bible teaches that love is a form of spiritual warfare.

Romans 12:21 says that we overcome evil with good. Romans 13:12 teaches us to put on the armor of light, and only light can dispel the darkness that prevails today. To live in the light is to live as Jesus lived, and He is love (1 John 4:8). He loves everyone with no exceptions—even those who are hard to love.

In Colossians 3:14–15, Paul urges us, "And above all these put on love, which binds everything together in perfect harmony. And let the peace of Christ rule in your hearts, to which indeed you were called in one body. And be thankful" (ESV).

What does it mean to "put on" love? It means to love *on purpose*. This sounds so simple if we would just do it—love people, live in peace, and be thankful. But we run into the problem that some people are hard to love, and too often we don't want to do what is hard, so we follow our emotions (feelings) and let the devil have his way. Then we complain about the conditions in the world and think someone should do something. But we rarely think *we* should be that someone.

If you are looking for an easy way to love people who are hard to love, I must tell you from the beginning that I don't know of one. But I can tell you that when we do something difficult because we love Jesus and want to obey Him, we not only please God but we grow spiritually, becoming more and more like Jesus.

I do believe the world's problems can be solved, but it will require each of us doing our part. It will necessitate our becoming peacemakers and being willing to make loving others a priority in our lives. This begins at home and spreads from there. I ask you here, in the introduction to this book, to apply its message to yourself, not merely to others. Be willing to see your own faults, not simply those of other people.

In this book, I hope to address from all sides the challenges of loving those who are difficult to love and to leave you with an intense desire to be a peacemaker and a lover of people. I want this to become your main goal in life. Being at peace with people is a part of loving them, so we could simply say that our goal should be to walk in love at all times.

Before we go further, let me close the introduction with these words from Jesus:

> A new command I give you: Love one another. As I have loved you, so you must love one another. By this everyone will know that you are my disciples, if you love one another.
>
> John 13:34–35

PART 1

Love Changes Everything

CHAPTER 1

The Greatest Thing in All the World

And now these three remain: faith, hope and love. But the greatest of these is love.

1 Corinthians 13:13

Before we can attempt to love people who are hard to love, we need to understand the importance of love and to know what love is and is not. Loving and being loved make life worth living. Love is the energy of life, and it is what motivates people to get up each day and keep going. Some people are motivated by making money, so they get up each day to climb the ladder of worldly success. Even though they may think they love what they do, they are loving something that can never fulfill or satisfy them. Anything apart from God has no ability to make and keep us happy.

Love is the energy of life.

Everything you take into your home is in the process of decay and will one day land on a junk pile somewhere, so don't place too much value on material goods. The apostle Paul writes: "We brought nothing into the world, and we can take nothing out of it" (1 Timothy 6:7). If you are spending your time trying to get more and more material possessions, I encourage you to think seriously about this verse.

Love gives life purpose and meaning. People in the world are looking for love, but they are really looking for God, because He is love (1 John 4:16). Love isn't something God does. It isn't something God gives to good people and withholds from evil people because He is love. He cannot do anything but love because love is *what* He is and *who* He is. While we were still sinners, He loved us and gave His Son to die for us (Romans 5:8).

The Russian writer Leo Tolstoy (1828–1910) wrote a story commonly called in English "Where Love Is, There God Is Also." It's the story of a shoemaker named Martuin Avdyéitch, a good man who suffered many difficulties, including the deaths of his wife and of all their children, except his beloved three-year-old son. One day, the son developed an illness, and after being sick for a week, he died. Overwhelmed with grief, Martuin stopped going to church.

One day an elderly neighbor man went to visit Martuin, and Martuin started complaining about all the bad things that had happened to him and saying that he wanted to die because he had nothing to live for.

The old man told Martuin that his problem was that he wanted to live for his own happiness. Martuin asked, "But what shall one live for?" The old man replied that we must live for God. He then told Martuin to buy a New Testament and read it because it would explain everything he needed to know about living for God.

Martin started reading the Bible only on holidays, but eventually read it every night. One night, he read in Luke 7:44–46 the story of Jesus' visit to the house of Simon the Pharisee. As he slept that night, Martuin had a dream that caused him to believe Jesus would visit his house, as He had visited Simon, the following day.

The next day, Martuin looked for Jesus, but when he looked out the window, he encountered only a weary neighbor shoveling snow. He invited the man into his warm house, gave him some tea, and enjoyed a conversation with him.

A bit later that day, Martuin looked out the window again and saw a woman and a crying child, poorly clothed and unable to stay warm in the winter weather. Martuin invited them into his home, led them to warm themselves by his fire, fed them, and gave the woman a coat and some money.

Next, Martuin looked out his window and saw an old woman struggling as she tried to sell apples. A little boy stole one from her, and Martuin convinced the boy to apologize and the woman to forgive him. Martuin then bought the boy an apple and sent him on his way.

When evening came, Martuin prepared to read his Bible and remembered his dream from the previous night. He heard footsteps behind him and a voice whisper to him: "Martuin—ah, Martuin! Did you not recognize me?"

"Who?" Martuin asked.

"Me," he heard a voice say.

The old man shoveling snow stepped up to Martuin, and the voice said, "It's I," then disappeared.

Then the woman and her child who were cold and hungry stood before him, and Martuin heard, "And this is I." Then they vanished.

Next, the old woman selling apples and the boy who stole from her appeared before Martuin, and a voice said, "And this is I."

Martuin looked at his Bible. He had opened it to Matthew 25:40: "Truly I tell you, whatever you did for one of the least of these brothers and sisters of mine, you did for me."

The story concludes with this: "And Avdyéitch understood that his dream had not deceived him; that the Savior really called on him that day, and that he really received him."

Tolstoy's story makes my point well. We often want God to visit us or to do some miraculous work to prove that He cares for us, but we can see from God's Word and this story that anytime we show love to another person, God is there.

Consider these scriptures:

> No one has ever seen God; but if we love one another, God lives in us and his love is made complete in us.
>
> 1 John 4:12

> God is love. Whoever lives in love lives in God, and God in them.
>
> 1 John 4:16

> Whoever does not love does not know God, because God is love.
>
> 1 John 4:8

True Love in Action

Matthew 25:31–46 tells us what will happen when Christ returns and separates the sheep (righteous people) from the goats (unrighteous people):

> He will put the sheep on his right hand and the goats on his left. Then the King will say to those on his right, "Come, you who are blessed by my Father, take your inheritance, the kingdom prepared for you since the creation of the world. For I was hungry and you gave me something to

eat, I was thirsty and you gave me something to drink, I was a stranger and you invited me in, I needed clothes and you clothed me, I was sick and you looked after me, I was in prison and you came to visit me."

Matthew 25:33–36

Then those on His right will ask when they did these things, and He will answer, "Whatever you did for one of the least of these brothers and sisters of mine, you did for me" (v. 40).

Next Christ will turn to those on His left and say that when He was hungry, thirsty, a stranger, in need of clothes, sick, or in prison, they did not look after Him (vv. 42–43). Jesus will say to them, "Whatever you did not do for one of the least of these, you did not do for me" (v. 45).

This story is impactful because it teaches us that Jesus considers the way we treat others to be the way we treat Him. Since this is the case, where does that leave all the people who are angry, filled with hatred, and selfish and who do nothing for those in need? We should remember that eternity is a very long time, and the way we live now determines where we will spend it. Will we spend eternity in heaven with God, or will we spend it in utter darkness and misery with the devil? God gives us all free choice, and we should choose to serve Him no matter what anyone else does. The choices we make now determine what our future will be.

> Jesus considers the way we treat others to be the way we treat Him.

Where does loving people fit into your list of priorities? Jesus said, "A new commandment I give to you, that you love one another; as I have loved you, that you also love one another" (John 13:34 NKJV). If we keep this one command, we will not sin, because love always puts God first and never does anything that will harm another person.

What Love Is Not

Knowing what love is certainly helps us learn to walk in love, but we are also wise to understand what love is not. Many people become confused about love because people tell them they love them and then act in ways totally inconsistent with real love. Love is not talk or theory, and it is not merely a sermon. It may produce feelings, but it is much more than a feeling, because we can love by choice even when the feeling of love is absent.

My father abused me and my mother abandoned me to the sexual abuse my father perpetrated on me, yet God asked me to take care of them as they got older. I will confess that I was never once excited to go to their assisted living apartment and eventually to the nursing home to visit them. I went because I knew it was the loving thing to do and that doing the loving thing, even to people who had abused and abandoned me, was something that God expected of me. I didn't feel like spending my hard-earned money on them, but I knew that love would have me take good care of my parents. Dave and I paid for them to live in a nice place rather than putting them in a cheap place where we knew they would not be well cared for. We bought their clothing, made sure they had groceries, took them to medical and dental appointments, and helped them in other ways.

We don't have to feel like doing the right thing in order to do it. This is what it means to love people who are hard to love. It means to treat them as Jesus would treat them, no matter how they have treated us.

When we decide to love people who are hard to love, feelings

of love may rarely be present. As I mentioned in the introduction to this book,
I think love can be described as how we
treat people. It is important to remember that we can love someone and not
like everything they do.

> When we decide to love
> people who are hard to
> love, feelings of love may
> rarely be present.

The Bible says that God does not show favoritism (Acts 10:34;
Romans 2:11). He gives everyone equal opportunity and loves
everyone the same, but each individual must choose how to
respond to Him. All prejudice and racial divides would disappear
if we all simply loved as God loves. Love sees the best in people,
and it is willing to pray about and be patient with the aspects of
people that aren't so good. Love always believes the best about
others.

Love is not selfish or self-centered, and it doesn't have to be
right. As a matter of fact, love sacrifices its right to be right. It
is not impatient or harsh. It does not gossip, criticize, or spread
rumors about the faults and sins of others, but it covers them and
prays for their forgiveness and change of heart.

The Bible says that love covers a multitude of sins (1 Peter 4:8).
The story in Genesis 9:18–27, about Noah and his three sons,
teaches us this lesson. The ark had finally landed on dry ground,
and Noah planted a vineyard. In due time, he made wine, drank
until he became drunk, and ended up lying naked in his tent.
His youngest son, Ham, saw his father's nakedness and told his
two brothers who were outside the tent (Shem and Japheth). They
placed a garment across their shoulders, walked into Noah's tent
backward so they wouldn't see their father's nakedness, and covered him.

When Noah awoke and learned what Ham had done, he pro-
nounced a curse upon him. But Noah praised Shem and Japheth

and declared that Ham would be a slave to them (Genesis 9:24–27).

Ham was Noah's youngest son. Often, young Christians who have no experience or spiritual growth make unwise decisions and act in foolish ways. Ham's behavior in this story was unwise, and it shows a lack of spiritual maturity. In 1 Corinthians 3:1, the apostle Paul refers to people who act unwisely as babies in Christ. He even mentions that they are babies because they are worldly, jealous, and quarrelsome (1 Corinthians 3:3). We can assess the maturity level of believers in Christ by watching their behavior. Ham showed spiritual immaturity, but Shem and Japheth showed spiritual maturity. When I was a young Christian, I was quick to gossip and spread rumors, but as I grew in God, I learned that this type of behavior displeases God.

God wants us to cover one another, rather than exposing people and spreading bad reports about them. Not gossiping is part of Christianity 101. Love does not gossip, because love treats others the way it wants to be treated.

Practice Loving Others

As we practice loving people on purpose, we develop the habit of loving others. Those who have practiced love and developed the habit of loving even when it is hard will automatically fall back on love in the situations and challenges they face. However, people who don't make a priority of loving will find that love is not their default behavior.

Years ago, when God showed me how selfish I was and I started trying to learn how to love people, I had to deliberately try to think about it all the time. Now that I have practiced love for years, I think about it without having to make much of an effort to do so. The same will happen to you. Anytime we form a habit, it is difficult at first. We do it and then we forget to do it, and after a while something happens and we remember again and do it for a while and then forget again. But if we don't give up and we continue praying and asking God for help, we will become more loving people.

Of course, we will always be growing in this fruit of the Spirit called love (Galatians 5:22–23). Paul's prayer for the Philippians was that their love would "abound more and more" (Philippians 1:9), and he encourages the Thessalonian Christians: "May the Lord make your love increase and overflow for each other and for everyone else" (1 Thessalonians 3:12). In other words, we cannot love too much and should always continue to find new ways to show love to other people.

If you want to love people, you will need to take time to listen to them and find out what they want and need. Do they need encouragement? Do they need financial help? Do they need to be included in family activities because they are single, widowed, or lonely? We usually assume that people need and like what we do, but we are all different and everyone feels loved in different ways.

> We cannot love too much and should find new ways to show love to others.

In his book, *The Five Love Languages*, Gary Chapman writes about five ways people give and receive love:

1. quality time
2. acts of service
3. words of affirmation
4. gifts
5. physical touch

I like gifts and acts of service. My husband likes quality time. One of my daughters likes encouragement, and one likes gifts and acts of service, as I do. One son likes gifts and one likes gifts and encouragement. Some people have more than one love language, as I do, but most people usually have a dominant one.

If you really listen to people, they will tell you what they want and need. They do this without realizing they are doing it. They are not hinting, but as you get to know them you will notice what they like, and you should be ready to love them in ways that they need to be loved.

> If you really listen to people, they will tell you what they want and need.

My husband loves sports, and I don't know or care much about them. In fact, sports would be the last topic I would love to have a long conversation about, but recently Dave and I went to lunch and I spent our time together asking him sports questions and letting him go on and on about the various qualities of different players and their records.

Loving people means doing what is for their good, not necessarily yours. Love is the greatest thing in the world. It has the power to change lives, and it defeats the devil in his works on the earth. Nothing gives people more joy than feeling loved. We can tell someone we love them, and it is meaningful, but when they *feel* loved, it is much, much better. People will always remember how you made them feel when they were with you, even if they forget what you said or did. Make people feel good about themselves and you will have many friends.

CHAPTER 2

Loving People Who Are Hard to Love

We Must Love People the Way They Are, Not the Way We Want Them to Be

Author Unknown

God takes us the way we are and helps us become everything we should be. The question is, are we willing to do this for other people? Dave did it for me, and had he not loved me unconditionally, I probably wouldn't be in ministry today. God wants to use people to help other people, and in order for Him to do so, we must be willing to love people who are hard to love. When Dave prayed for a wife, he asked God to give him someone who needed help, and God certainly answered his prayer, because I needed *a lot* of help.

Many years ago, I shopped at a grocery store that featured a cart containing cans of food that were dented or missing their labels. Everything in the basket cost ten cents, but if you bought a can without its label, you had no idea what you would get.

At that time, we were always short on money, so I would buy several cans hoping for peaches, applesauce, canned vegetables, or something else our family would enjoy. Occasionally I got something good, but sometimes I got dog food, cat food, or something we would never eat. Dog food may have been a blessing to some people, but we didn't have a dog, so it wasn't good for us.

When I chose dented cans, of course, I got the ones with the smallest dents. I believe we often take the same approach with people, because in certain ways they are much like those dented and unlabeled cans. Everyone comes with some dents in their personality, some characteristics we may not view as positive. In addition, people are not always labeled, so to speak, which means we may think we are getting one thing and end up with something entirely different. I can hear many people saying, "Amen to that."

> People are not always labeled.

My grandson recently looked at a house he considered buying because he could afford it. The house wasn't expensive, but it came as is, meaning that if he bought it, he didn't know how many problems he was also buying. Of course, he and his dad looked the house over carefully to find its faults, and they found one with the foundation—a large crack that had been repaired but looked as though it might still leak during rainy weather. They decided against buying the house, which was probably a wise decision.

The story about dented and unlabeled cans of food and the house my grandson considered buying illustrate the way I was when Dave married me. I had lots of dents and faults, but I had covered them up well. I also came with no label, and although Dave fell in love with me quickly, he had no idea what he was getting. I had a crack in my foundation, because during the formative years of my life, I endured sexual and mental abuse from my father and had a mother who didn't know how to deal with it, so she simply ignored it.

The situation with my parents was probably the most difficult life experience I have faced when it comes to forgiving people who have hurt me. My father did not apologize to me until he was eighty years old. Thankfully, he also accepted the Lord at that point in his life. My mother apologized to me thirty years after I left home at age eighteen, and she asked me how I felt about her. I wanted to be truthful with her, so I told her that I didn't love her as a girl should love her mother, but that I did love her as a child of God and that I would always make sure she was well taken care of. I followed through on that promise. I had truly forgiven her, but as you will read several times in this book, forgiveness is not a feeling. It is a decision we make about how we will treat the people who have hurt us.

The abuse during my childhood seriously affected my personality. I was controlling and afraid, but I pretended not to be fearful. I had a root of rejection (meaning that I was predisposed to think people would reject me or were rejecting me even when they weren't), and I was filled with shame, condemnation, insecurity, and many other negative issues. I also had an anger problem and felt the world owed me for the injustices I had suffered.

> Forgiveness is a decision we make about how we treat people who hurt us.

When Dave and I had been married about three weeks, I had a temper tantrum over something minor. He looked at me and asked, "What is wrong with you?" He had begun to realize that under the surface something was indeed wrong.

Several years passed before I realized something was wrong with me. Until that time, I thought everyone else had problems and that, if those people would simply be more like I was, we could get along. Have you ever thought that if someone you were in relationship with were more like you, things would be so much better? Have you tried to change them and failed time and time again?

While Dave and I were dating, I looked and acted normal, and I must have been on my best behavior. Because we had only five dates before he asked me to marry him, he didn't have much time to see the real me. He said he knew the first night he met me that I was the girl for him. As it's turned out, he was right, but he had to be willing to love someone who was very hard to love for a very long time before he had a wife who was somewhat normal.

I think few men would have done what Dave did, because most people are too addicted to their own comfort to be willing to suffer in order to give God time to heal another person. But Dave is a godly man, and an unusually patient one, and he learned early in our relationship to enjoy the parts of me that were enjoyable and turn the ones that weren't over to God. He knew he couldn't change me, so he prayed for me and went about enjoying his life.

Enjoy What You Have While You're Waiting for What You Want

I believe a key to being able to love someone who is hard to love is to enjoy the good parts of that person while you are waiting for God to deal with the bad parts. You may think, *Joyce, there are no good parts of the person I am dealing with.* But this simply isn't true, because everyone has some good qualities. If we have focused on their negative aspects consistently for a long period of time, we may no longer see the good parts, but they are there if we really look for them.

> Enjoy the good parts of a person while waiting for God to deal with the bad parts.

God wants us to enjoy our life,

and being miserable because someone else has problems doesn't help them or us. I was unhappy, but Dave wouldn't let me make him unhappy. Although this infuriated me, it also helped set me free. People with dents and cracks (issues) usually want to drag others down to their level so they can feel better about themselves. However, if you don't let them do so, they just might change eventually. Unhappy people want to make other people unhappy too.

Dave did for me what God has done for us in Jesus. Romans 5:8 says, "But God shows and clearly proves His [own] love for us by the fact that while we were still sinners, Christ (the Messiah, the Anointed One) died for us" (AMPC).

Dave was so loving and peaceful that I eventually wanted what he had and got serious enough in my relationship with God to begin facing my issues and receiving healing.

When you find yourself faced with someone who is hard to love, thinking about how God loved you when you were hard to love will help. The first step toward loving people who are hard to love is to pray for ourselves to have a godly attitude and to remember that God loved us when we were hard to love.

I think most of us are hard to love in some way. We are often frustrated with other people's minor faults while we have major faults we do not see in ourselves. The busier we stay dealing with the flaws in other people, the less likely we are to see our own. The devil's strategy is to keep us so busy finding fault with others that we never recognize our own problems. The truth is that we cannot change other people. But we can cooperate with the work the Holy Spirit wants to do in us when we face the truth about ourselves, repent, and ask God to change us.

> The first step in loving people is to pray for ourselves to have a godly attitude.

Porcupine People

We give children almost every kind of stuffed animal, even alligators, which I think are ugly, but I've never seen a stuffed porcupine for sale, nor a child who owned one. Children may enjoy looking at them, but no one wants to cuddle up with a porcupine.

In the animal kingdom, probably the most difficult animal to get close to is the porcupine. Porcupines are not usually considered loveable, but they do manage to get together once a year for mating season. Every porcupine has about thirty thousand sharp quills that can stick you and be very painful and even dangerous. These quills are their way of protecting themselves.

Likewise, people develop ways of protecting themselves, especially if they have been hurt in the past. Sometimes, our methods of self-protection come across as odd to people who are dealing with us. For example, a person who has been hurt may be extremely defensive and think they are being rejected when that is not the case at all. Or they may argue all the time, striving to be right in every situation because that is the only way they can feel good about themselves.

I know a few people who are like this, and I call them "porcupine people." You probably know some too. They are dangerous to be around because you are likely to get hurt. You may never know it if you don't get close to them, but if you do get close enough, you will eventually see their dents and cracks and feel their jabs. It would be so nice if we could just place an order for the kind of people we would like to have in our life, but people come as is, and we either take them as they are or end up alone.

I was a porcupine person, but I try hard not to be one anymore. I pray regularly to be good to people and make them feel good when they are around me. I'm sure I don't always succeed, but I don't always fail either. I still stick out my quills occasionally, but God is working with me, and I always want to be willing to work with the porcupine people He puts in my life too.

You may have heard the old story about porcupines needing to get close to each other in order to stay warm during a bitterly cold winter. They have to choose between being cold or being stuck occasionally by another porcupine's quills. In the end, they choose to put up with being stuck, and they all survive the winter.

This is a good lesson for all of us. We may sustain little wounds from time to time as we walk through life with other people, but we are much better off in relationships than in isolation.

Desire

You will never be able to love people who are hard to love unless you have a strong desire to do it for God and in obedience to Him. I know this from my experience with my parents. They never gave me a reason to love them, but they gave me many reasons not to. So when God asked me to take care of them in their old age, providing for them and making sure they had a good life, it was one of the most difficult times for me to say yes to Him. But it surely wasn't even close to how difficult it must have been for Jesus to suffer and die for our sins. If we call Jesus Lord, there are two words we can never say to Him: "No, Lord." If He asks us to do something and we say no, then although He is our Savior, He is not our Lord. When He is our Lord, we say yes.

> If we call Jesus Lord, there are two words we can never say to Him: "No, Lord."

You have to want to please God more than you want to please yourself, and if you can do so, He may use you to change someone's life. I am living proof that this works, and I don't even want to think about how miserable my life would have been had Dave said no to God. He could have bailed out of the situation at any time, but he stayed. He has shared that he often sat in his car and cried because he simply did not know what to do. I'm so sorry I hurt him so much, but I am so glad he did not give up on me.

Having a desire to please God doesn't mean we will enjoy loving people who are hard to love. Remember, love is much more than a feeling. It is how we treat people. God isn't asking us to let people abuse us, but He is asking us not to give up on them simply because they are difficult to deal with. There are times when we cannot be with certain people because they are abusive, but we can still pray for them and love them in ways that won't put us in harm's way. These are rare cases, and most of what we are talking about in this book pertains to ordinary people who for a variety of reasons are just hard to love.

> God asks us not to give up on people simply because they are difficult to deal with.

It Started in the Very Beginning

People having flaws and faults is nothing new. All you need to do is read Genesis—the first book of the Bible, often referred to as "the Book of Beginnings"—to realize that. One of the earliest recorded stories in Genesis is about Cain (Adam and Eve's first son), who killed his brother, Abel, because he was jealous of him (Genesis 4:8). Throughout the book of Genesis, we see everything from polygamy to incest, drunkenness, lying, Joseph's brothers wanting to kill him, and Abraham having sex with his wife's servant (Genesis 4:19; 16:1–4; 19:30–38; 27:1–35; 37:18–20).

The people involved in these situations are people God used, so I guess this means there is hope for us.

It seems like if we are going to love anyone, it will have to be flawed people who are sometimes hard to love. But remember that we are flawed, have many faults, and are often hard to love also. Love is the greatest thing in the world, and it changes everything. Just imagine how different our world would be today if people truly loved one another. Is this possible? I would like to believe it is. In the natural realm, apart from God, it may be unlikely, but the Bible tells us that all things are possible with Him (Matthew 19:26). When we get to heaven, it will be a definite reality for us as believers, as we will enjoy an atmosphere of perfect peace and love.

I can't know or be responsible for what everyone else does, but I have decided that I am going to love people, and by God's grace, this includes people who are hard to love.

I am asking you to make the same decision, and I believe that if enough of us do it, it will impact the world in a very positive way.

> Let your behavior be a sermon that people cannot ignore.

Practical Steps to Loving People Who Are Hard to Love

- Don't simply *try* to love them or assume you can love people who are difficult for you to love. Pray regularly that God will give you the grace to do so. Lean on God for His help, because without Him you will surely fail.
- Pray for the people who are hard for you to love. Ask God to reveal truth to them and change them. Ask Him to soften their hard hearts.

- Be a good example. Instead of trying to talk people into changing, let your behavior be a sermon that they cannot ignore forever.
- Be ready to forgive often—at least as often as God forgives you. Forgive them not because they deserve it, but because you deserve peace.
- Don't broadcast their faults or mistakes by spreading rumors or speaking negatively about them.
- When the opportunity arises, bless them in a practical way or help them when they have a need.
- Set an example. Treat everyone with kindness and respect, even those who are rude to you—not because *they* are nice, but because *you* are.
- Don't gloat (secretly rejoice) when they have trouble or misfortune.
- Be prepared to be patient, because truly loving them may take practice and perhaps longer than you would like.
- While you are waiting for your breakthrough, make good choices by treating other people the way you would like to be treated.
- Remember that what others say and do and the opinions they express are based almost entirely on their own self-reflection. Don't take things personally. Instead of becoming angry over people's words, choose to grow stronger because of them.
- Remember the saying "Hurting people hurt people." There is a reason people behave the way they do, and it is usually not because they want to. They are either deceived and don't realize what they are doing, or, like I was, they are merely acting out their own hurt or modeling behaviors they observed or were taught while growing up.

- Learn to ignore the drama, discouragement, and negativity surrounding you. Don't let it limit you or stop you from being the best person you can be.
- Don't let other people's behavior determine how you behave.

> Remember the saying "Hurting people hurt people."

Tough Love

Loving people doesn't mean that we never confront them, but we should do so only as God directs and not just when we want to. While Dave was waiting for God to change me, there were times when he confronted me, but after the confrontation he continued to love me. He never once shut me out of his life or mistreated me because of my behavior. Those times of confrontation were very difficult for me, and I usually reacted in anger, but Dave wouldn't argue with me. His silence gave God time to work with me and help me see that Dave was right.

Dave remained the same no matter what I did. This is how God is, and it should be our goal too. He never let me drag him down to my level of behavior, but instead he provided me with an example to which I could aspire.

I realize that each person's situation is very different, and setting guidelines that will perfectly fit every situation is impossible. But if we are willing to follow His lead, God will guide us individually and customize a plan for everyone we deal with.

Can I promise that if you do what I suggest that the person who is hard to love will change? No, I cannot make that promise, because their will is involved, and ultimately they must make a choice. But even if they never change, you will be blessed because you are doing what God wants you to do, and that is the most important thing you can do.

People Are Starving for Love

I don't believe there is a person on the planet who doesn't want to be loved. As a matter of fact, most people who are hard to love are the way they are because they have never experienced real love. They are dissatisfied and looking for something to fill the emptiness they feel, but often they don't know what they are looking for, so they search for it in all the wrong places. Each time they think they find what they long for, they end up disappointed, and it only makes their behavior more challenging for those around them.

> Most people who are hard to love have never experienced real love.

We can love God only because He first loved us (1 John 4:19), but when we have His love in our hearts, we can let it flow through us to other people. Everything God gives us should flow through us to others—His love, peace, kindness, mercy, forgiveness, joy, and many other blessings.

Loving people who are hard to love will be difficult on most days and seemingly impossible on some days, but God never asks us to do something without giving us the ability to do it with His help. Don't listen to the lie that it is just too hard, because if you believe it is too hard, it will be. You can do it because God is in you and He will do it through you. Are you willing to say yes to God?

CHAPTER 3

The Character of Love

Dear children, let us not love with words or speech but with actions and in truth.

1 John 3:18

Words of love are good, but actions of love are better. Love can be seen and felt in many ways, and it has specific character traits. Paul writes to the Corinthian believers:

Love endures long and is patient and kind; love never is envious nor boils over with jealousy, is not boastful or vainglorious, does not display itself haughtily. It is not conceited (arrogant and inflated with pride); it is not rude (unmannerly) and does not act unbecomingly. Love (God's love in us) does not insist on its own rights or its own way, for it is not self-seeking; it is not touchy or fretful or resentful; it takes no account of the evil done to it [it pays no attention to a suffered wrong]. It does not rejoice at injustice and unrighteousness, but rejoices when right and truth prevail. Love bears up under anything and everything that comes, is ever ready to believe the best of every person, its hopes are fadeless under all circumstances, and it endures everything [without weakening]. Love never fails [never fades out or becomes obsolete or comes to an end].

1 Corinthians 13:4–8 AMPC

Each quality Paul mentions in this passage is a character trait of love and should be individually considered and practiced. Remember: practice makes perfect. The more we practice a skill, the better we become at it. Practice love and you will begin to excel at loving others.

Let's take time to look at the various characteristics of love in 1 Corinthians 13:4–8 so we will understand each one and grow in our ability to express it.

Love Is Patient

Love can be seen and felt as we are patient with the weak and erring. Most people in the world today are in a hurry and don't even know what they are hurrying to do. But the hurry habit causes us to be impatient with others, especially if they make mistakes or don't move as fast as we would like them to move. We want people to be patient with us and actually become offended when they are not. But we are not always willing to give to others what we want them to give to us.

> We are not always willing to give others what we want them to give to us.

I want to confess that impatience of this kind is my biggest weakness. I have prayed about it for years, and I am growing, but I still have a long way to go. Writing this book is good for me because I am seeing some things about myself as I write, and thinking about them to share them with you will help me love people more.

Patience is long-suffering. It doesn't give up easily. Patience is a fruit of the Holy Spirit that only grows under trial. We are usually reluctant to pray for patience because it means an increase in situations that will require us to be patient. The apostle James describes a patient person as "mature and complete, not lacking anything" (James 1:4). This means patient people are totally content with their current circumstance because they trust God and believe He always has a plan that will ultimately benefit them.

Without patience, it is hard to love people who are easy to love and basically impossible to love those who are hard to love. Some people never change, and in order to love them, we must be willing to put up with the same flaws over and over again, just as God does with us. It seems that God always manages to put in our lives some people who have traits that frustrate or irritate us.

> Without patience, it is hard to love people.

I am a bottom-line person and can usually say what I want to say in a few words, yet still get my point across. This means I am impatient with people who want to tell me every tiny detail of a story or situation. Dave is a detail person, and it takes him a long time to tell me what he wants to communicate. If he wants to tell me about a movie that he watched, I know I am in for a long, intricate story, but I realize that listening patiently will make him feel loved.

I am a rather serious person who has a lot of responsibility, and I am usually thinking about something I need to do, teach, or write, so I can become easily annoyed with people who want to goof around too much, especially if I am in work mode. But, once again, if I want to love them, I need to be patient. Barbara Johnson said, "Patience is the ability to idle your motor when you feel like stripping your gears."

Though love compels us to accommodate others at times, we don't always have to adjust to do what someone else would want us to do. In my life, I may encounter someone who is eager to play and have fun and doesn't understand the responsibility I have on a particular day. I don't have to throw away my responsibility and do whatever the person wants, but I can lovingly explain that I have things to think about and take care of that are important, and that today I need to be more serious-minded. If the person loves me, they will understand that and want to provide what I need.

The closer a relationship is, the more important it becomes for us to know what the other person in the relationship needs and wants and to provide it as often as possible. I mentioned in a previous chapter Gary Chapman's book *The Five Love Languages*, which explains this principle in detail and is worth reading.

Some people don't seem to have a love language, but I know they do; we simply have to look for it. It took me a long time to identify Dave's love language. If I asked him what it was, he had no idea. But eventually, with some help from our children, I realized it was quality time. Love is giving people what *they* need, not what *we* need. So, when I want to show love to Dave, I need to listen to him and let him tell me the long version of what he has done or seen.

Love Is Kind

Kindness is selfless, compassionate, and merciful. It cannot be earned, because it is a gift and can only be received with gratitude. When we are kind to others, we do for them things they have not earned or deserved. If we want to see a picture of kindness, all we need to do is look at Jesus.

We often talk or hear about random acts of kindness. This means doing something nice for someone we may not even know and who certainly has not done anything to earn the kindness we may demonstrate to them. The world is a harsh place, and it is our privilege as children of God to show kindness to others.

> It is our privilege as children of God to show kindness to others.

Some people do not know how to receive kind acts of grace because they have spent their life trying to earn everything they get. Kindness is given graciously and should be received the same way. God is kind. He gives to us far more than we deserve and often withholds punishment that we do deserve. William Penn said, "I expect to pass through life but once. If, therefore, there be any kindness I can show, or any good thing I can do to any fellow being, let me do it now, and not defer or neglect it, as I shall not pass this way again."

Let me encourage you to take every opportunity that comes your way to show kindness, for it truly is one thing people need most. It melts hard hearts and heals wounded ones. When we do something kind for someone for no reason except to be kind, it carries a power that can change the world. Just imagine how different the world would be if everyone were kind to one another. It would surely be wonderful. You can make a difference in a life today by simply being kind.

Love Is Not Envious or Jealous

Love rejoices when others are blessed rather than being envious or jealous of them. A person who loves trusts God to give them what is right for them at the right time. They are not in competition with anyone else, because they are secure enough not to need to compare themselves with others. Robert Heinlein said, "A competent and self-confident person is incapable of jealousy in anything. Jealousy is invariably a symptom of neurotic insecurity."

According to Proverbs 14:30, jealousy and envy are strong

enough to rot our bones. That doesn't sound good, does it? The best way to avoid jealousy and envy is to admit when we feel it, confess it to God, and ask for His help right away. We can even take some aggressive action and buy the person we are jealous of a nice gift just to let the devil know we refuse to live according to his wicked ways. We can and should also pray for the person to succeed in all they do.

Love is something we must seek, pursue, and put on intentionally. We can't simply wish we felt loving toward someone; we must be determined to love, love, and love some more. People experience jealousy when they are afraid that someone else will get ahead of them, look better than they do, have something they want, be more popular they are, or cause them to lose some type of status that they have. But the truth is that if we trust God, no one can take away anything God wants us to have.

> If we trust God, no one can take away anything that God wants us to have.

You may remember King David, mentioned in the Bible, and Absalom, his son. In trying to take the kingdom from David, Absalom worked behind David's back to gain favor with the people (2 Samuel 15:1–12). Absalom eventually won the hearts of the people, and David had to flee from the city with his household.

He said, "Take the ark of God back into the city. If I find favor in the Lord's eyes, he will bring me back and let me see it and his dwelling place again. But if he says, 'I am not pleased with you,' then I am ready; let him do to me whatever seems good to him" (2 Samuel 15:25–26).

Absalom ended up riding a mule under the thick branches of an oak tree. His hair got caught in the tree and the mule went on, leaving Absalom hanging in the tree, where he was eventually killed by Joab and his men (2 Samuel 18:9–15). David had continued to walk in love toward Absalom no matter what he did, and he mourned his death as though Absalom had done nothing to wrong him (2 Samuel 18:33–19:4). We can see that instead of becoming jealous, David left the situation to God, knowing that Absalom could not take the kingdom unless God wanted him to have it.

Those who know how to trust God save themselves a lot of heartache. They walk in love, knowing that God will always do what is right and best for them and understanding that no one can take what God wants them to have.

I admit that I feel jealous sometimes, but I am determined not to put up with it, because I know it is not pleasing to God and is foolish on my part. I pray against it, and soon it goes away. It is nothing more than a ploy of the devil to try to make me miserable and to prevent me from loving the person who is being blessed. Jealousy keeps us focused on what we don't have and prevents us from being thankful for what we do have.

Love Is Not Proud or Boastful

Simply put, love doesn't think more highly of itself than it should, because people who walk in love don't spend much time thinking about themselves. Their minds aren't on themselves, but on how they can bless other people.

The humble person has no problem saying "I'm sorry" or "I was wrong," but the proud find these words difficult to utter. Pride wants to be seen, to be first, and to know more than others do. It seeks to be noticed and admired, frequently gives opinions, and thinks it is right in every debate. Pride always comes before destruction, but humility comes before honor (Proverbs 16:18).

People who are proud boast of their accomplishments and talk incessantly about all they are doing. They rarely, if ever, give any credit for their success to God or anyone else. God will humble the proud, and it will not be comfortable for them. But if people are willing to humble themselves under the mighty hand of God, He will lift them up at the right time (1 Peter 5:5–6).

Love does not boast of its own accomplishments because it knows it could accomplish nothing without God and without the people God gives to help. Love delights in giving credit to others and in making them look good. The better we make someone else look, the better we look to others. Humility is a beautiful quality, and when we have it, people admire us for it. Humility gives to us what we try to get for ourselves through pride without success.

> Love delights in giving credit to others and in making them look good.

Pride was the sin that caused the devil to be kicked out of heaven (Isaiah 14:12–15), and it is truly the root of all sin. Pride always says "I": "I want," "I need," "I did," and "I will." Love is not proud, because love is concerned with the welfare of others, while pride only cares for itself. Humility is probably one of the most difficult fruits of the Holy Spirit to maintain because Satan always whispers, "What about you?" He tempts us continually to think about and be concerned about what will happen to us. He tries to convince us that if we don't take care of ourselves, no one will, but this is not true, because God will always take care of us if we trust Him to do so.

God wants us to take care of others while He takes care of us. If we give Him that opportunity, we soon realize that He takes better care of us than we could ever take care of ourselves. Thomas Merton said, "Pride makes us artificial and humility makes us real." Samuel Butler said, "The truest characters of ignorance are vanity and pride and arrogance."

Love Is Not Rude

Rudeness is, sadly, one of the hallmarks of our world today. People push to get ahead no matter who they hurt along the way. *Please* and *thank you* are rarely in their vocabulary. They take the parking place you are waiting for, leave messes for others to clean up, throw trash out of their car window, interrupt people when they are talking, and other such things. They speak harshly to those who are being patient with them, or they lack compassion when others are hurting. Simply put, they just don't care about others. They think only of themselves and don't consider whether their behavior hurts or injures someone else.

I know a few people who have excellent manners, and being around them is so refreshing. When I am with them, the entire atmosphere seems to be good. Parents should take the time to teach their children good manners, but a lot of the problem is that children today are learning from parents who had parents who did not teach them good manners.

Common sense teaches us that if we want other people to like us, we need to have good manners. Even if no one taught them to you, you can learn from God's Word, and if you find someone with good manners, you can learn from them too.

Good manners show consideration and respect for others. Be willing to learn good manners and begin to practice them. In fact, I recommend researching good manners on the internet. You will find many good examples of the proper ways to behave.

Love Is Not Self-Seeking

Self turns inward, but love flows outward. One of the main signs of the end times is selfishness, and we certainly see it in the world today. There is nothing wrong with doing things for ourselves. In fact, I encourage people to do so. But if that is all we do, then it is wrong. We should be serving, giving, and doing all we can to make other people's lives better.

> It is impossible to be selfish and happy at the same time.

It is impossible to be selfish and happy at the same time. If all I have room for in my life is me, I will live a very narrow life and be very unhappy. Being unselfish may be the most difficult facet of love to develop, but with God's help we can do it.

I frequently catch myself being selfish. I want to eat where I want to eat, not where Dave wants to eat, or I want to watch what I want to watch on TV instead of what he wants to watch. I want to buy the piece of furniture I like, not the one he likes. It hurts to admit these things, but confession is good for the soul. I'm not where I need to be, but thankfully I am not where I used to be.

Jesus says that if we want to be His disciples, we must forget and lose sight of ourselves and our own interests and take up our cross and follow Him (Mark 8:34).

> Unselfish living must be sought after every day of our lives.

The cross we are asked to carry is living unselfishly. It sounds easy, but it isn't. Unselfish living must be sought after with ardent zeal every day of our lives. John 15:13 says, "Greater love has no one than this, that someone lay down his life for his friends" (ESV).

Perhaps we can begin with one unselfish act each day and build from there. When we have spent a lifetime trying to make ourselves happy, we probably cannot conquer selfishness all at once. But we can conquer it with God's help. He has told us to love and that love is not selfish, so with His help it is possible to become an unselfish person.

Love Takes No Account of the Evil Done to It

I would have to say that many people in the world today are touchy and easily offended, but love doesn't behave that way. It never holds a grudge, but quickly forgives, just as God does. At one time in my life, I kept records in my head of everything anyone had done to hurt me. I could list them anytime I became angry, but love has taught me to let go of things as quickly as possible. Always remember: The more quickly you let go of an offense, the less likely it is to take root in your soul.

> The more quickly you let go of an offense, the less likely it is to take root in your soul.

Don't let negative memories poison your soul. They will only make you unhappy and prevent you from being able to love people. Bitterness makes all of life bitter, but love makes it better.

Even people who are easy to get along with will hurt us at times, and we must be able to quickly let go of pain and offense, or we will open a door for the devil to torment us. Let's practice being the kind of people who are almost impossible to offend. I don't want to waste any more of my time being angry, upset, or offended due to being touchy, and I'm sure the same is true of you.

I want to say again: The best way not to remember the evil that has been done to you is to forget it as quickly as possible. Don't keep a mental list and keep reminding yourself of the things that have been done to you, or you will never get over them. God forgives and forgets our sins, which is what we should do in our dealings with one another. Another helpful strategy is to believe the best, instead of the worst, about people in every situation.

Love Always Believes the Best of Everyone

This facet of love enables us to do what I just mentioned: let go of hurts and offenses. How can we forget the pain people cause us unless we are willing to believe the best of them? The question is always, Did that person hurt me on purpose, or did I get hurt because I am touchy? Often when people hurt us, it is because they are hurting and don't even realize how their actions affect others.

God's Word teaches us not to offend or to take offense (Proverbs 19:11; Matthew 5:23–24). Two people have a responsibility, but if one refuses to do their part, it does not alleviate the other person's responsibility to do theirs. If someone does something intending to offend me, it doesn't mean I have to take the offense. Later in the book, you'll find an entire chapter on offense, because the Bible says that one sign of Jesus' imminent return is that many people will be offended, and we need to know how to deal with it.

> Believing the best of people prevents us from wasting energy on anger.

Believing the best of people prevents us from wasting energy on anger that isn't necessary. We can choose to believe the best about someone just as we can choose to believe the worst. We can be suspicious, or we can be positive and trusting. Of course, we tend to think we don't want to let anyone get away with hurting us and not protect ourselves, but on the other hand, we can trust God to protect us since He promises to vindicate us (Psalm 35:23–24).

Wise people do what they can do to enjoy their life, and choosing to believe the best is something we can do that will help us live joyfully, peacefully, and with a sense of purpose. The things that happen to us are not as important as our perspective of them. The way we look at people or circumstances is very important, because a positive perspective can turn a bad situation into a good one.

If you have been hurt in the past, it may have caused you to be suspicious of people, and you may assume they intended to hurt you. I understand that feeling, because I was that way. At one time my attitude was "You can't trust anyone." However, God has taught me that having that perspective is a miserable way to live. Now I would rather trust people and be wrong occasionally than be suspicious all the time and miss relationships or experiences with people who are trustworthy. Someone said that suspicion is the cancer of friendship. We cannot be foolish and assume that no one will ever hurt us, but neither should we be suspicious and assume that everyone will hurt us. I urge you to believe the best, for you will be a much happier person if you do.

Love Does Not Rejoice at Injustice and Unrighteousness

Love grieves over injustice. People who love always want what is fair and right not only for themselves but also for others. Love doesn't like to see people mistreated. We should care about others and their pain, and we should pray for them diligently. We should also do whatever we can do to relieve their suffering. Love cannot look at unjust situations and simply not care.

Through the media, we hear of murder, rape, mass shootings, and every kind of violence. We hear of domestic abuse, starvation, natural disasters that ravage people's homes and lives, children who are trafficked for sex, and many other horrific situations. We may not be able to fix everyone's problems, but we can care and we can make sure that we don't allow our hearts to become hardened by the frequency of these reports. We can all do something, and doing something will make a big difference. We can financially support ministries and organizations that help these victims, and we can volunteer to help them however we can. I pray that I never get so accustomed to hearing of injustice that it no longer touches my heart.

Love Never Fails

The kind of love that God has bears up under anything that comes. This love has been poured into our hearts by the Holy Spirit (Romans 5:5), and it endures everything without weakening. It is determined not to give up on even the most difficult people. My father was one of the meanest people I've ever known, but love finally melted his hard heart, and before he died, he was born again and lived at peace for three years. Forgiving him and loving him was not easy, but it was easier than hating him. I thank God

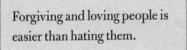

Forgiving and loving people is easier than hating them.

for giving me the grace to walk in love, because truly, love did not fail.

It is difficult to keep showing love to someone who never seems to appreciate it, but we are not responsible for how others act; we are only responsible for our own actions. Make the decision to do what is right no matter what anyone else does, and you will be a happy person. Don't fail to walk in love, because love never fails.

PART 2

Love and Peace in Relationships

CHAPTER 4

Becoming a Peacemaker

Silence is a great peacemaker.

Henry Wadsworth Longfellow

Peace and love are the two main qualities the world needs today, and just as each of us is responsible for walking in love and even loving people who are hard to love, we are also responsible for being peacemakers. Jesus says, "Blessed are the peacemakers, for they will be called children of God" (Matthew 5:9). According to this scripture, God's children should all be peacemakers. Let me encourage you to take an honest assessment of yourself and ask yourself if you are a peacemaker. You might say, "Well, I'm not a troublemaker." But are you a peacemaker? Part of loving others is to be willing to go the extra mile to make peace when there has been trouble between you and them.

When trouble comes in my life, I may not be the one who starts it, but will I work to bring peace to the situation? Doing so often requires humility and a willingness to be silent, as the opening quote of this chapter recommends. To be a peacemaker, we may have to let someone think we are wrong and say nothing to defend our point of view. There is a time to speak and a time to be silent (Ecclesiastes 3:7), and we need the wisdom to discern the difference.

Humility and peace work together, and both are attributes of wisdom (James 3:13–18). Paul encourages us to live in harmony with one another and writes that a humble mind is necessary to do so (Philippians 2:2–5). Humility helps us avoid petty arguments (2 Timothy 2:23–24). There are times when we need to confront issues, but we must also learn not to be petty or waste our energy on unimportant matters.

Wise people walk in peace; they are makers and maintainers of peace. In our world today, we see much violence from people who are fighting for justice. They feel they have been mistreated and demand that people treat them differently, but peace never comes through violence. Martin Luther King Jr., Nelson Mandela, and Mahatma Gandhi are all great examples of people who fought for justice but did so through peaceful protests, not violence.

Jesus, the Prince of Peace

Jesus is referred to as the Prince of Peace (Isaiah 9:6). He brought peace wherever He went because He had peace inside of Him. In Mark 4:39, He could speak peace to the storm raging outside only because He had peace on the inside. I frequently say, "We cannot give away what we don't have," and we cannot bring peace to situations if our minds and emotions are in turmoil.

Only those who are spiritually mature can be peacemakers, because keeping the peace requires us not to live according to our feelings. If our goal is to keep ourselves comfortable and happy, or to get our own way all the time, peace will be impossible.

Not long before Jesus appeared before Pilate and was sentenced to be crucified, He said, "Peace I leave with you...Do not let your hearts be troubled and do not be afraid" (John 14:27). The Amplified Bible, Classic Edition translation of this scripture says that not letting our hearts be troubled and not being afraid means we are to stop allowing ourselves "to be agitated and disturbed." Peace is available to us; we simply have to be willing to do whatever is necessary to enjoy it. Jesus gives us peace, but we are responsible for maintaining it.

> Jesus gives us peace, but we are responsible for maintaining it.

When we receive Jesus as our Savior and begin to live with and for Him, one of the first blessings we usually experience is peace.

Pursue Peace

I think it's safe to say that peace is hard to come by and even more difficult to maintain. Almost daily, Satan arranges circumstances that will steal our peace unless we are determined to hold on to it.

I grew up in a household that was anything but peaceful. I didn't even really know what peace felt like until I was in my forties. After getting serious in my relationship with God and beginning to study His Word, I prayed for peace, but it always seemed to elude me. God finally taught me that I was praying for peace when I needed to be pursuing it.

God's Word teaches us to pursue peace—to seek it, crave it, and go after it (1 Peter 3:11). We are to pursue, seek, and crave peace with God, peace with ourselves, and peace with others. In the Amplified Bible, Classic Edition, Colossians 3:15 teaches us to let peace be the "umpire" in our lives, meaning to let peace make the final decision regarding what we do or don't do. If you have peace, then follow it. If you don't, then wait to make a decision until you have peace about what to do. Make peace one of your top priorities in life.

As I mentioned earlier, much of this book is about love and peace because they are so important but missing from our society today. Satan works diligently to rob us of our peace. I say he sets us up to get upset. He arranges circumstances that annoy us, hoping to steal our peace. He also finds people through whom he can work to upset us. But we can defeat him if we will hold on to the peace Jesus left us. How important it is to do so!

Ephesians 6:10–18 teaches us how to effectively wage spiritual warfare and fight the devil in ways that allow us to win our battles and maintain our peace. God's methods and strategies for victory are quite different from the world's ways. According to His Word, to win the spiritual war, we are to walk in truth, put on righteousness, and put on shoes of peace, meaning to walk in peace (vv. 14–15). We are to take up the shield of faith to "extinguish all the flaming arrows of the evil one" (v. 16), and we are to put on the helmet of salvation (v. 17), so we can think as a child of God should think.

In addition, we are told to take up the sword of the Spirit, which is the Word of God (v. 17). This means we need to speak the Word during times of trouble, because it defeats the devil. When the devil lied to Jesus, Jesus responded, "It is written," and then He quoted Scripture to refute the lies Satan tried to convince him to believe (Matthew 4:1–10).

Lastly, Ephesians 6:18 tells us to cover everything with prayer and to pray at all times with "all kinds of prayers and requests." Prayer should always be our first line of defense against any problem we face.

> Prayer should always be our first line of defense.

As you read at the beginning of this chapter, Henry Wadsworth Longfellow said, "Silence is a great peacemaker." When Jesus was accused of things of which He wasn't guilty, He held His peace and kept silent (Matthew 26:59–63). Trying to defend ourselves to people who are already determined to hurt us is a waste of time. If they have their mind made up, then God is the only one who can change it. This is why praying for them is better than trying to convince them. When we pray, God works, but when we work without God, He waits.

Keeping quiet when we are falsely accused is difficult to do. One of our basic instincts is to defend and protect ourselves, because we want people to think well of us. But God is our Defender, and we should pray and wait on Him unless He instructs us to take action.

Let me say again that we have to pursue peace, seek it, crave it, and go after it with all our might. We cannot simply pray for it, wish for it, or hope we have it; we must pursue peace and be determined to take peace everywhere we go.

Peace with God

Peace must begin with God. We cannot have peace with ourselves or anyone else until we are at peace with God. This requires obedience to His will and repentance of our sin when we do not obey Him.

As long as people continue to do things their conscience condemns, they will never enjoy peace. It is foolish to fight against God, because we will either learn to live His way or we will be miserable. People who continue to behave in ways they know to be wrong will never have peace, and if they don't have peace, they cannot be peacemakers.

> As long as people do things their conscience condemns, they will never enjoy peace.

Making peace with God is easy. All we need to do is confess and admit our sin, and God promises to forgive us, forget the sin, and never bring it up to us again. Jesus has already paid for all our sin, and He is just waiting for us to accept His forgiveness. We cannot sin more than God's grace can forgive. Where sin abounds, grace does "much more abound" (Romans 5:20 KJV).

Peace with Yourself

I have found during my years of ministry that many people don't like themselves, let alone love themselves in a balanced way. I certainly started out this way. I was ashamed of myself because of the abuse I had endured, and I didn't like myself, so I couldn't have peace with myself. Even though the abuse was not my fault, I still felt guilty most of the time. There were, of course, times when I did sin and feel guilty about it, but often I simply struggled with the general feeling that something was wrong with me.

If you don't like yourself, then you are miserable, because you never get away from yourself. Everywhere you go, you are there. To love yourself simply means that you have accepted God's love for you. I am not suggesting that we be in love with ourselves, be selfish, and think only of ourselves, but we do need to have a healthy attitude toward ourselves and appreciate what God did when He created us.

To not like ourselves can be insulting to our Creator. He created each of us carefully and intricately with His own hand (Psalm 139:13–15). He does not make mistakes, and we need to receive the love He offers us as a gift. We cannot earn or deserve it, but we can receive it and be thankful for it.

We see our flaws and know the mistakes we have made in the past, and this can often cause us to struggle to let go of them and move on. We try to change ourselves and end up frustrated because only God can change us. He has begun a good work in us, and He will complete it and bring it to its finish (Philippians 1:6). God knew when He created us that we would make mistakes and sin. Otherwise, we would not need Jesus.

We should all do the best we can and cooperate with the Holy Spirit's work to mature us spiritually, but we are not perfect, and although we are changing all the time, we make mistakes. When Jesus, the Perfect One, returns, then we shall all be changed "in the twinkling of an eye" (1 Corinthians 15:52). We must remember that although people see and judge us according to what they see or experience of us on the surface, God sees our heart. I believe we can have a perfect heart toward God, but we won't have perfect behavior until we are no longer in our flesh-and-bone bodies.

We must all accept ourselves where we are and celebrate the progress we have made while God is still changing us little by little, or as Scripture says, "from glory to glory" (2 Corinthians 3:18 NKJV). The good news is that we can enjoy ourselves and enjoy our relationship with God while we are changing.

> We can enjoy ourselves and enjoy our relationship with God while we are changing.

Let me ask you: What is it that you don't like about yourself? If you can change it, then do so. If you cannot change it, then pray about it, study what God's Word says about that aspect of your life, and trust God to do the work in you that needs to be done. Don't focus on your flaws. The more you think about them, the bigger they will seem. Perhaps you don't like the way you look or your personality, but that is probably because you are comparing yourself with someone else. Each of us is unique and precious in God's sight, and we should not compare ourselves to anyone else. The fact that you are not like other people in no way means that there is something wrong with you.

We all do things wrong, but we also do things right.

For example, I am still impatient in some instances. When that happens, I repent and ask God to forgive me. But I am also very generous. I love to give, and generosity is one of my motivational gifts. I cannot sing or play a musical instrument, but I am a good communicator and Bible teacher. I still recognize selfishness in myself at times, but I am merciful and forgiving. The same principle applies to you. You have weaknesses and strengths, and you should be fully aware of both. Knowing what your strengths are isn't wrong or arrogant; it's good and healthy.

We are to look away from everything that distracts us and look to Jesus, "who is the Author and Perfecter of faith" (Hebrews 12:2 AMP). Constantly looking at our faults distracts us, prevents us from growing spiritually, and keeps us from doing what God wants us to do. We should not deny our faults, nor should we focus on them excessively.

Coming to terms of peace with yourself is important in order for you to enjoy your life, but it is also important to the people you come in contact with. If you don't have peace with yourself, you will never be able to maintain peace with anybody else.

How Your Thoughts Affect Your Peace

Our thoughts affect our words and our behavior. We cannot have peace in our lives if we don't think peaceful thoughts. I highly recommend thinking thoughts on purpose rather than just waiting to see what falls into your mind and thinking about that.

I like to encourage people to think power thoughts, which are thoughts that add power to your life and strengthen you rather than stealing your power and making you weak. If you want to be a peacemaker, you can begin by spending some time each day thinking a peace power thought and saying, "I am a peacemaker.

I work for peace everywhere I go. I avoid all strife and disunity."
As you do this, you are renewing your mind, which will help you
see yourself in a new way. As soon as you believe you are a peacemaker, you will begin to be one.

Another powerful tool in your arsenal is God's Word. If you are
serious about pursuing peace, get on your computer or use a Bible
concordance and look up every scripture you can find about peace.
Read them over and over again until they become part of you.

Be willing to work hard in order to have what you want. Lazy
people never have victory. Be aggressive and do your part to fight
the good fight of faith. We can wish for peace, but that will never
bring it into our lives. We have to insist on having peace and do
whatever we need to do to see that happen.

When someone does something you don't like and you immediately start thinking about all the qualities you don't like about
that person or to the ways they irritate you, change your thoughts
and believe the best of them, as love would have you do. We never
know what people may be going through to make them do what
they do. Pray for them immediately. It is
difficult to stay angry with someone you
are praying for.

> It's difficult to stay
> angry with someone
> you are praying for.

God's Word says, "We have the mind of
Christ" (1 Corinthians 2:16). Since this is
true, we must be able to think the same way He thought. Admit-
tedly, developing new thoughts or habits takes time, but there is
no better time to begin than right now.

Find Your Peace Stealers

We all have our peace stealers—things that regularly upset us—
and it is important for us to know what they are. What kinds

of situations steal your peace? Which people in your life irritate you most? What is it about them that annoys you? I ask these questions because being aware of what bothers you can help you avoid being upset and help you not fall into the same trap over and over again.

Awareness gives you an opportunity to pray about things. Don't just ask God to change the people and circumstances that irritate you; ask Him to change you and make you more tolerant. Ask Him to help you maintain a good temper in the midst of circumstances that try your patience. Look for the positive aspects of people instead of focusing only on the qualities you view as negative. Look for and focus on the blessings—not just the challenges—in your life.

One of my peace stealers is rushing. I have to make an effort to leave enough time to do what I need to do without getting into a hurry. In addition, I've always been a hard worker, so lazy people annoy me, and I have to remember that we are not all alike. I'm aggressive, so passive people frustrate me. I want them to make a decision and do what they need to do without making excuses about why they aren't doing it, but once again I need to remember that we are not all alike. I have just as many faults as anyone else, just in different areas. Most of us tend to judge people who are not strong where we are strong, but God tells us in His Word not to judge others so that we will not be judged (Matthew 7:1). Romans 2:1 tells us that we do the same things we judge in others. We see their faults, and of course we assume there is no excuse for their behavior, but we are quick to make excuses for ourselves.

> We don't have to worry. We can pray instead.

Worrying steals anyone's peace, but we don't have to worry. We can pray instead.

> Do not be anxious about anything, but in every situation, by prayer and petition, with thanksgiving, present your requests to God. And the peace of God, which transcends all understanding, will guard your hearts and your minds in Christ Jesus.
>
> Philippians 4:6–7

This is my go-to scripture when I start to worry. I meditate on it and speak it aloud until I calm down. God's Word is filled with power, and it will help you if you will use it as He intends.

I have a strong faith in the power of prayer because I have seen what God will do when we pray. I have learned that one prayer can do more than years of worry, which does nothing except wear me out, make me difficult to get along with, give me headaches, and steal my joy.

Some other things that I am aware of that can steal my peace (and perhaps yours also) are being double-minded instead of making decisions and sticking with them, trying to figure things out when only God has the answers, and refusing to forgive people who have hurt me. Letting myself get too hungry can make me irritable. My computer can upset me when it gets a mind of its own and won't work when I am in the middle of a project I need to finish, and my printer tries my patience when it gets jammed with paper and I can't seem to fix it. All the technology we have available is wonderful until it doesn't work, especially if you're like me and are not technology-minded enough to fix it. Not minding my own business also robs me of my peace. Sometimes the less we know about a situation, the more peaceful we can be.

When I allow circumstances or people to steal my peace, I'm learning to take a deep breath and say, "Joyce, stay calm, because getting upset isn't going to change anything." It's all right if you talk to yourself. Sometimes I have to talk myself off the ledge, so to speak. I will be on the verge of jumping into a situation that will steal my peace and I talk myself out of it.

Perhaps reading about my peace stealers has helped you identify what regularly upsets you. Let me encourage you to make a list of things that regularly steal your peace. Determine that with God's help you will not let those things control you, but that you will choose peace.

What Is the Value of Peace?

Living in peace is Kingdom living. God's Kingdom doesn't consist of possessions or earthly treasures, "but of righteousness, peace and joy in the Holy Spirit" (Romans 14:17). We are not living the life Jesus died for us to have if we don't have peace. If something isn't valuable to you, then you won't do what you must in order to have it. So ask yourself, "How valuable is peace to me?" Do you want it enough to make whatever changes you need to make in order to have it?

> We are not living the life Jesus died for us to have if we don't have peace.

Are you willing to join the army of peacemakers God needs in order to turn the tide of the lack of peace in the world today? We can make a big difference if each of us will simply do our part. Let peace begin in your heart and in your home and spread from there. If you decide to join the peacemaker army, you need to know that not everyone will be willing to be at peace with you. But as far as you're concerned, be at peace with everyone (Romans 12:18).

CHAPTER 5

The Danger of Anger

Fear is the only true enemy, born of ignorance and the parent of anger and hate.

Edward Albert

I think this chapter's opening quotation gives us insight into what is happening in the world today. We know that more than ever people are angry, and many are actually filled with hatred toward those with whom they are angry. The results of the 2019 NPR-IBM Watson Health Poll reveal that 84 percent of those surveyed said that people in the United States are angrier today than they were a generation ago.

I have two granddaughters who work at a fast-food restaurant, and they have told me stories about how angry people become if they don't get their food quickly enough or feel they didn't get enough ketchup packets. These girls and others who work with them have been threatened, cursed, and screamed at, and they have watched adults act worse than any toddler having a temper tantrum. These people are probably not angry about their food; they are simply angry and explode every time something doesn't go the way they want it to. They may be angry about something entirely unrelated to their food order, but they take it out on anyone who irritates them. They are like pressure cookers ready to blow at any moment.

Perhaps people's anger is rooted in fear: fear that they won't get what they want, fear of being mistreated or overlooked, fear of injustice, fear about the condition of the world, fear due to financial concerns, fear for their children, fear of being taken advantage of, and all kinds of other fears.

"Perfect love casts out fear," according to 1 John 4:18 (NKJV). When we know that God loves us, we don't have to be afraid. And if we are not afraid, we won't be angry and filled with hatred.

Anger can also be due to hurts or injustices people have experienced. Many people are angry today because they feel they have been treated unjustly in the past. They may be right, but anger won't change the situation. Prayer, forgiveness, peace, and love are much more powerful than anger.

> Prayer, forgiveness, peace, and love are much more powerful than anger.

What are people angry about? I think they instinctively know that something is terribly wrong in the world, and they don't know what to do about it, so they look for someone to blame, someone to be angry with. People are angry with the news, the president, and other politicians. If they are poor, they may be angry with the rich. They may be angry with a culture or race that is different from theirs. They may be angry with their job—the pay, the working conditions, or a promotion they thought they deserved but didn't get. People are also angry about injustice, or at least what they perceive as injustice.

Underneath all the reasons we can list, I think the real reason people are angry is that they are trying to live without God in their life. Or if they do say they believe in God, they are not serving and obeying Him. The problem with anger is that it solves nothing, and I can say without hesitation that if everyone loved and obeyed God, we would have none of the problems that we face in the world today.

God's love takes away our anger when we are in right relationship with Him. The world is a violent place, and it is impossible to solve our problems with violence. Love is the only answer,

> God's love takes away our anger when we are in right relationship with Him.

and love understands that violence can never bring peace. Martin Luther King Jr. said that love is the only power that can turn an enemy into a friend. He also said, "One day, we must come to see that peace is not merely a distant goal we seek, but that it is a means by which we arrive at that goal. We must pursue peaceful ends through peaceful means."

The Bible includes at least two great examples of men who were angry due to fear, both of them involving people who felt threatened by King David. In the first story, David's brother, Eliab, had seen Samuel anoint David as Israel's future king (1 Samuel 16:1–13). Because Eliab wanted that position for himself, he became jealous, and his jealousy turned to hatred and anger (1 Samuel 17:28).

I think Eliab was also afraid that David would look better than he did or be more popular than he was. After all, Eliab was a soldier, and he was older than David. I am sure he felt entitled to receive the anointing and to be chosen as king. But God looks at the heart, not the outward person (1 Samuel 16:7), and He saw in David the heart of a great leader for His people.

When a battle broke out between the Israelites and the Philistines and David went to see what was going on, Eliab began to verbally belittle him. In fact, 1 Samuel 17:28 says that "he burned with anger" toward David, and asked, "Why have you come down here? And with whom did you leave those few sheep in the wilderness? I know how conceited you are and how wicked your heart is." David ignored Eliab, which is exactly what we should do when people try to make us feel incapable and unable.

In the second example of fear that led to anger, King Saul, who reigned as king when David was anointed, was so angry with David that he repeatedly tried to kill him. His anger was rooted in fear and jealousy that David would take his throne prematurely. Saul knew that he had disobeyed God and that he would lose the throne because of it. David was very popular with the people, and Saul's anger mounted to a fever pitch. It seemed that all he could do was think of killing David (1 Samuel 18:6–12, 29).

It is amazing what fear and jealousy can do to a person, but being angry doesn't solve our problems or prevent God from doing what He intends to do.

Is Anger a Sin?

The Bible teaches that we can be angry without sinning (Ephesians 4:26–27). Feeling the emotion of anger is not a sin, but what we do with our anger can become a sin if we don't handle it properly. The scriptures in Ephesians that say "be angry and do not sin" (Ephesians 4:26 ESV) also tell us not to let the sun go down on our anger, nor to allow anger to give any foothold to the devil.

If you are angry with someone, the best course of action is to humble yourself and call or visit the person and apologize. Even if you don't think the altercation was your fault, you can still take steps to be a peacemaker. The word *anger* is only one letter away from *danger*, and it does not promote the righteousness that God desires. James 1:19–20 teaches us to be "quick to listen, slow to speak and slow to become angry."

One of the best ways I know to manage anger is to deal with it right away, because the longer we wait, the angrier we may become. I encourage you not to let anger stay in your heart long enough to take root. Remind yourself of how useless it is and remember that it is not pleasing to God. Look up and read every scripture on anger you can find. If you have an anger problem, put some of these scriptures on a card, on a piece of paper, or in your phone, where you can access them quickly when needed. Read, meditate on, and speak them. Let the Word of God, which is the most effective tool you have, work for you.

Some people simply cannot manage their anger alone, and if you are one of them, I would encourage you to seek professional help. Whatever you do, don't let anger control your life.

My father was an angry man, and I can testify that he had a miserable life and made most of the people around him miserable also. Angry people often end up being lonely people. Sooner or later, those around an angry person will grow weary of dealing with them and find friends who are more pleasant.

> Angry people often end up being lonely people.

Solomon, who was called the wisest man in the world, writes that anger lodges in the heart of fools (Ecclesiastes 7:9). He also writes, "He who is slow to anger is better than the mighty, he who rules his [own] spirit than he who takes a city" (Proverbs 16:32 AMPC). This is quite a statement if we stop and think about it. Do you consider yourself to be a person of good sense? If so, then you will rule your spirit, meaning restrain your anger. This doesn't mean you will never feel angry, but that you will restrain your emotions or use self-control.

What about your friends? Are they peaceful people or angry people? God's Word encourages us not to make friends with angry and hot-tempered people and not even to associate with one who is easily angered (Proverbs 22:24–25). Why? Because we might become like these people if we spend too much time with them.

A few days ago, I was sitting at a red light. When the light turned green, the man in the car behind me immediately honked his horn. People are impatient and very much on edge these days. They seem ready to explode at the slightest provocation, and I am sure that the devil loves it.

Are You Angry with Yourself?

Are you angry with yourself because of mistakes you have made? If so, there is nothing you can do but repent, let go of the past, and press forward. If you don't, you will end up wasting the rest of your life.

Many people who don't use self-control are angry with themselves. They see that their lives are in a mess, and they know it is their own fault. But instead of doing something to turn their situation around, they simply feel guilty and beat themselves up with their attitude about what they should have done but didn't do. It is never too late to begin doing the right thing.

> It is never too late to begin doing the right thing.

People-pleasers become angry with themselves because they have let other people control their life and make their decisions for them. They are angry because they have been weak. But once again, just being angry doesn't solve anything, it only makes us miserable and often causes us to hurt other people. You can take your power back and start making your own decisions, led by the Holy Spirit. The people who have been controlling you won't like it, but you must decide if you want to be happy yourself or continue keeping them happy.

If you are angry with yourself, anger will come out of you and express itself toward other people. You will find fault with them or come up with a reason to direct toward others the anger you

> If you are angry with yourself, anger will come out of you and express itself toward others.

actually feel toward yourself. First Peter 3:11 says that we are to be at peace with God, ourselves, and our fellow human beings (AMPC), and I believe peace must come in that order. We must have peace with God first, then we can have peace with ourselves, and finally we can have peace with other people. We can love people, even those who are hard to love.

Are You Angry Because Your Life Hasn't Been Fair?

Much of the anger we experience in the world today is due to one issue: the fact that many people feel their life has not been fair. Some people feel that they have not been treated well in the past, and they intend to collect on what they think is due them. I understand this feeling, because I've felt it myself. As someone who was sexually abused, I felt I was owed something, but I tried to collect from all the wrong people. I looked for compensation from people who could never pay me back. Even my father, who was my abuser, could not give me back what he had taken from me. Only God could pay me back, and only God can pay you back.

If you are trying to collect on past pain and injustice, please turn all your injustice over to God ask Him to be your vindicator. He will give you double blessings for your former trouble, and He is the only one who can do it.

> Turn all your injustice over to God.

Instead of your [former] shame you shall have a twofold recompense; instead of dishonor and reproach [your people] shall rejoice in their portion. Therefore in their land they shall possess double [what they had forfeited]; everlasting joy shall be theirs.

Isaiah 61:7 AMPC

Before you can move beyond anger, it is important to locate the source of it. Are you angry with a person who mistreated you? The world's system? A family member? An abuser? A friend? Life in general? Are you angry because your life didn't turn out the way you thought it would? Are you angry with God because you asked for something and didn't get it? If you are angry, who are you angry with? Name your anger, let go of it, turn it over to God, ask Him for justice, and move on with life. Every day that you put off doing this is a day that perpetuates your misery, because angry people are miserable people.

Are You Angry and You Don't Know Why?

Some people are angry and don't even know what the root cause of their anger is. I was one of those people. I thought that because I got away from my father when I turned eighteen years old and left home, I left the problem behind me. But I actually took it with me in my soul. I carried it around for years, not knowing what it was. It made me sad, angry, dissatisfied, discontent, and unable to love, and led to many other dysfunctions. I struggled with these but was clueless about their cause.

The first step I had to take toward freedom and peace was to own the anger. I had to admit that I was an angry person and that I tried to use my anger to control the other people in my life. I asked God for help, and gradually I began to see that my behavior was rooted in my childhood and that I had to deal with it. Anything we run from continues to chase us. I was running from the truth, but it was only the truth that could make me free (John 8:32). I had to face the fact that my parents did not know, nor would they ever know, how to love me, but that I had a Father in heaven who loved me more than anyone on earth ever could.

As I have mentioned, I was sexually abused. I could not go back and undo that, but I could give it to God and ask Him to work it out for my good, based on Romans 8:28. I didn't have to see myself as a victim, because when I received Jesus, the old me died and a brand-new me was recreated in Christ (2 Corinthians 5:17).

Repressed Anger

There is expressed anger, and there is repressed anger. The anger we express is not hidden. We know it is there, and other people know it too. But repressed anger has been pushed down for so long that we don't think we are angry. We may have other problems that actually stem from repressed anger, but they are not the real issue. We may be critical, negative, sour, and cynical. We may have a bad attitude, be jealous, or struggle with an eating disorder, an addiction to drugs or alcohol or gambling, or many other dysfunctional behaviors. We can deal with the fruit of these, and even if we conquer one, another will pop up until the repressed anger is dealt with. It is like playing the old arcade game Whac-A-Mole, in which a mole would pop up and you would hit it on the head with a mallet, only to find it quickly pop up in another place.

Real freedom only comes when we get to the root of our problems and allow God to heal all our wounds and bruises.

> But He was wounded for our transgressions, He was bruised for our iniquities; the chastisement of our peace was upon Him; and by His stripes we are healed.
>
> Isaiah 53:5 NKJV

> He heals the brokenhearted and binds up their wounds [curing their pains and their sorrows].
>
> Psalm 147:3 AMPC

> Real freedom comes when we allow God to heal our wounds.

These scriptures and others similar to them got me through a lot of hard days while God was working in my life to help me overcome my past.

God wants to use you to heal others, but a wounded healer isn't very effective. Let Him heal your wounds first, and then you will have firsthand knowledge and experience to share with others.

Anger is dangerous if it isn't dealt with, so be sure that you don't just ignore it, thinking that as long as you hide it, it won't be a problem.

Righteous Anger

Only one kind of anger is good, and that is righteous anger. We can feel a righteous anger toward sin and at the same time feel mercy toward those who commit sin. We are to hate what God hates, and He hates sin. But He loves those who sin and works with them toward repentance and restoration.

Jesus expressed righteous anger when He went into the temple and overturned the tables of the money changers (Matthew 21:12–13). Jesus also became angry because of the hardness of the Pharisees' hearts (Mark 3:1–6). In 2 Chronicles 28:25 and

33:6, God displayed righteous anger when He became angry with idol worship and witchcraft. Righteous anger is always handled properly.

I feel righteous anger when children are abused, when people mistreat other people, when people go hungry and homeless, and when I see other ways people struggle or suffer. But my solution to the anger is to try to do something about the problem. Simply being angry does no good, but working toward peaceful solutions does. We should feel a righteous anger at injustice. The best way to handle injustice is to work for justice.

If you are angry, it is time to own your anger, ask God to help you get to the root of it, and deal with it. Instead of being an angry person, you can have peace in your own heart and be a peacemaker in the world around you.

CHAPTER 6

Disagree Agreeably

We may disagree on some things, but we can do so without being disagreeable.

Christine Gregoire

We typically find loving people who don't agree with us more difficult than loving those who do. When everyone around us agrees with us and thinks as we think, loving them is much easier. Respecting everyone's right to their own opinion is an important key to loving people. When we try to convince people to change their mind and agree with us, if we continue doing it long enough, it usually ends in anger. People want freedom; they don't want control and manipulation.

> People want freedom, not control and manipulation.

The way we treat people with whom we disagree is important. Life is too short to argue and be angry and unforgiving. We don't all agree, but we can learn to disagree agreeably.

Dave and I have certainly had to learn how to disagree agreeably to stay married fifty-five years. We are two very different people, and there are things that are important to me that are not important to him. Likewise, some things that are important to him are not important to me. If we try to decorate a home together, it simply doesn't work because I want everything to match and blend, and Dave wants everything to stand out. We found a place of agreement when we moved into our current home and he agreed to let me decorate the house while I agreed to let him have the biggest office with the better view.

In the earlier years of our marriage, I simply couldn't understand how Dave could think the way he thought when his perspective or opinions did not agree with mine. But I have since learned that we all see things from different perspectives. If we want to have peace in our relationships, respecting everyone's right to their own opinion is very important. When we respect that right, we don't argue with them about what they think, or make comments that make them feel that something is wrong with them because they feel the way they do. We may have discussions over topics or situations about which we don't agree, but a discussion is not the same as an argument.

Learning to disagree agreeably is rooted in respect, and it is one of the most important skills we must learn if we want peaceful relationships. It seems that, in our world today, many people try to force others to think as they think, but that only creates a strife-filled atmosphere that fuels anger and even violence. For example, I know someone who is doing something that is definitely sin according to God's Word. Although I agree they have a right to choose how they will live, it doesn't satisfy them. They want me to agree that what they are doing is right.

> Learning to disagree agreeably is rooted in respect.

The idea that so many people want others to condone what they do or how they think is part of the problem in our society today. People want the right to make their own decisions and choices, but they get angry if you don't agree with what they are doing, and even go so far as to say you are guilty of a hate crime simply because you don't agree with their choice.

I do not hate anyone, and I do believe that each person has the right to free choice. God has given us that right. I also believe the Bible is the Word of God. It is what I live by, and I'm not going to agree that someone's choice is right if God's Word says it isn't. Let me clarify: I agree that a person has a right to make their own choice, but they don't have a right to try to force me to agree with them. In such instances, we can agree to disagree and still remain cordial with one another, with no strife between us.

There are thousands of issues about which people can disagree. Politics in the United States, for example, is a hot topic. Some people are staunch Democrats and others are staunch Republicans, and countless people argue about which viewpoint is right. They practically exhaust themselves trying to convince people to think like they think. Religion is another topic that people often argue about and that even destroys friendships. We should find subjects we can agree on and let those be the ones we discuss. It is permissible to discuss anything as long as we can do it peacefully and respectfully. If we cannot, then we should simply agree not to discuss it. Is politics really worth ruining a relationship over? I don't think so, because there is good and bad in both political parties.

Even When You Think You Are Right, You Could Be Wrong

Dave and I learned years ago to say, "I think I'm right, but I could be wrong." Learning to approach people this way, of course, requires some humility, but it puts an end to many arguments and saves a lot of relationships. These are nine powerful words that disarm the evil spirit that is trying to bring division among people. The truth of the matter is that many times we are positively sure that we are right and yet we end up being wrong, so why not admit that could be the case instead of insisting that we are right?

I recall an incident when Dave and I were driving to a friend's home and trying to remember where it was. We didn't get exact directions because we both *thought* we remembered how to get there. Dave thought we should go one way and I thought we should take another route. I argued my point so vehemently that he followed my suggestion.

I told him, "The house is up this street in a cul-de-sac." While driving up the street, I saw a bicycle and proudly proclaimed that I remembered seeing that same bicycle on a previous visit to our friend's house. However, when we got to the top of the street, there was no cul-de-sac and our friend's house was not there.

I was positive that I was right about the location of our friend's house, but I was wrong. Has that ever happened to you? I'm sure it has, and if it has then it could happen again, so why not take the high road and just say ahead of time, "I could be wrong"?

You will be amazed at how many arguments these words will prevent.

Pride Destroys Relationships

Pride goes before destruction, a haughty spirit before a fall.

Proverbs 16:18

Pride causes the destruction of relationships and destroys unity. It is impossible to argue over who is right unless pride is present. Humility works wonders in relationships, and I would encourage you to simply humble yourself under God's mighty hand and ask Him what

> Humility works wonders in relationships.

you can do to make your relationships better. Pride waits for the other person to make the first move, but humility is willing to take the first step, no matter who is at fault.

John Ruskin said, "It is better to lose your pride with someone you love rather than to lose that someone you love with your useless pride." Andrew Murray said, "Pride must die in you or nothing of heaven can live in you."

When I wrote in chapter 4 about the different facets of love, I noted that one of them is that love is not haughty and inflated with pride. Love is humble and always seeks what will bring restoration and peace. When you argue with someone about who is right when there is a difference of opinion, would it really be that difficult to say, "I could be wrong"? Surely not.

Being right is not as exciting as you might think. The feeling of exaltation it gives us lasts only a few moments. Then we have to face all the damage done to the relationship for the sake of those few

> Being right is not as exciting as you might think.

moments of feeling like we won, when the truth is that, in God's eyes, we lost.

When two people disagree about a decision that must be made, the one who is in authority should be the one to make it. In our ministry, each department has a manager. Everyone in the department may be involved in a discussion about something, but the manager is the one who must ultimately make the decision, and everyone else should respect their responsibility to do so, without strife or offense.

In our family, there was a time that Dave wanted to give some money to an organization to which I didn't want to contribute. I gave him my reasons for the way I felt, but he still felt strongly about giving the money, so I said okay. He is ultimately responsible to provide for our family, so I left the decision to him. I wasn't going to argue with him, especially not about giving.

Humility Wins in God's Eyes

Before Satan fell and became our enemy, he was an angel. But he rebelled against God and got kicked out of heaven to live eternally in hell. What was his sin? Pride, as I mentioned earlier. He declared that he would lift his throne above the throne of God (Isaiah 14:13), and no one can do that—not even an angel. Humility waits on God, but pride moves in its own timing and tries to get for itself what only God can give.

According to 1 Peter 5:6, we are to humble ourselves under God's mighty hand, and He will lift us up in due time. If we find ourselves in a situation in which we need to be shown to be right, God can easily arrange that. Humble people have no problem believing or saying, "I could be wrong," but proud people don't think they are wrong, nor would they admit it.

Jesus was humble, and Paul writes in Philippians 2:5–8 that we should let the same humble mind that was in Jesus be in us. Even though He was equal with God, He didn't think He needed to argue with those who accused Him of things of which He was not guilty. He had no need to prove who He was. He took on the role of a servant, and only a humble person can do that.

Insecurity and the Need to Be Right

Perhaps we fight to be right because we are insecure and being right makes us feel better about ourselves. The more secure I have become in Christ, the less I feel the need to prove I am right during conflict. Insecurity is the root of many of our problems.

It causes us to compare ourselves with others and compete to be better than they are or to look better than they do. It causes fear and prevents us from doing many things we would like to do or know we should do.

If people are insecure, they usually look for security in all the wrong places—perhaps in their work, or knowing the "right" people, or what they own, or their degree of education, or having others agree with their opinions. Yet, even if they have all of these, they will still feel insecure because true security can only be found in Christ Jesus, not in anything else. Paul teaches us to "put no confidence in the flesh," but only in Christ (Philippians 3:3).

When people are secure, they have less conflict with other people simply because they have nothing to prove. Jesus never argued with anyone, trying to prove He was right about anything. During His time in the wilderness, Satan tempted him in various ways. Two of those temptations involved trying to get Him to prove He was God's Son (Luke 4:3, 9). Both temptations failed because Jesus knew who He was, where He had come from, and where He was going.

> We are never truly free until we feel no need to impress anyone.

We are never truly free until we feel no need to impress anyone. If and when we reach that point, then we can rest internally and live without concern about what people think of us. We know that what they think is between them and God, and that what they think cannot hurt us. It is what we think of ourselves that really matters.

Like many people, I was insecure for years, but as I received God's unconditional love and acceptance, I found security in Christ. The better we feel about ourselves, the less we feel the need to argue over opinions and fight to be right, and we can find a way to disagree agreeably if the other person is willing to do so. Some people won't be at peace no matter what we do, but we can all be peaceful in and through Jesus.

A Wrong Opinion Doesn't Make You A Wrong Person

I am more than my opinion and so are you. We can be wrong about what we think, but that doesn't make us wrong as human beings. However, when someone's identity is tied to how well they perform in life, being right is much more important to them than it should be. Quite often, I think I'm right about something and that Dave is wrong, only to find out I was wrong and he was right. But being wrong doesn't change who I am.

Most of our family is fairly opinionated. We probably offer our opinions more often than we should, but we all forgive quickly and refuse to harbor strife. I am working on keeping my opinion to myself unless someone asks for it. I am "baby-stepping" toward victory, but it doesn't matter how slowly I progress as long as I am progressing.

Peace Is More Valuable than Being Right

Peace is wonderful! I enjoyed a totally peaceful day yesterday and recorded it in my journal. I hope to reach the place where every day can be that way, but I know I cannot reach this goal without humility and the willingness to let go of the need to be right all the time. The peace is worth the sacrifice to me because no matter what we have, if we don't have peace along with it, everything else is worthless.

To me, having peace is worth withholding my opinion and not

needing to have the last word in a disagreement. It is worth saying, "I may be wrong," or even "I am wrong." And it is worth saying, "I am sorry," or "Please forgive me."

I remember how totally miserable I was the last time Dave and I had an argument over a difference of opinion. I was so upset that it actually made me feel bad physically for two days. Even after we both said, "I love you," it still took time for my emotions to calm down. I can tell you that what we argued about wasn't worth the price I paid emotionally and physically to defend my opinion. Love gives up its right to be right, but I forgot that momentarily—just long enough to get into trouble and say the wrong thing at the wrong time.

Let's imagine for a moment what our world would be like if everyone would do what I have written about in this chapter and if, when they fail, they would quickly apologize and get back into peace as soon as possible. This is a lofty goal, but as I have said before, if each one of us will do our part it is possible, because all things are possible with God (Matthew 19:26).

What's Right for You May Not Be Right for Someone Else

Just because something is right for me doesn't mean it is right for everyone. We all like to do things different ways. Some people love to tell us how to do everything, based on how they do it and think it should be done. "I think" are two words we should say a lot less than we do.

> "I think" is something we should say a lot less than we do.

This is especially true once our children become adults. When they are grown, we must stop trying to run their lives if we want to have good relationships with them. This transition is very difficult for some parents to make. Their degree of pride determines how much or little they can mind their own business. We have spent eighteen years or so telling our children what to do and what not to do, and to suddenly stop doing that is challenging. We may offer an opinion if our adult children are open to one, but we should never try to force what we think is best on them. What was right for us may not be right for them.

Our intention may be to help them because we don't want them to make mistakes and hurt themselves. But they want to be free just as we did when we grew up and left home.

I urge you to let your adult children make their own decisions unless they want you involved and to allow them to deal with the consequences of the decisions they make, good or bad. We often learn more from our mistakes than we do from our successes, so even if they make a mistake, God can work it out for their good.

If you need to let go of trying to control an adult child, why not make today the day you do it? Waiting will only cause more arguments. You can learn how to disagree agreeably and respect-fully. Respect their right to make their own decisions even if you don't agree with them.

Work for peace and unity in all your relationships and love everyone. Even when people are hard to love, love them anyway, just as Jesus does.

CHAPTER 7

Avoiding Strife

Two aged men, that had been foes for life, / Met by a grave and wept—and in those tears / They wash'd away the memory of their strife; / Then wept again the loss of all those years.

Frederick Tennyson, "The Golden City"

Over the years, I have come to understand that strife is bickering, arguing, heated disagreement, resentment, bitterness, and an angry undercurrent. Strife is very dangerous, like a cancer that keeps spreading until someone stops it. Many people don't even know what strife is until it is explained to them, so they live in strife-filled atmospheres and experience its devastating effects, unaware that it is the source of their problem.

I was once part of a great church that was growing rapidly. It was filled with people who had tremendous potential, several of whom went on to be in full-time ministry. Sadly, those people were not sent out from that church because it was destroyed by strife. The leadership began taking the church in a direction many of the members did not agree with, and the congregation murmured and complained to one another. As the definition of strife says, there was an angry undercurrent in the church. This same dynamic exists in many homes, businesses, and churches. Strife leads to destruction, which will keep spreading unless people recognize and stop it. The only way to stop the strife is to confront the problem or the people causing it in a godly and loving way. The writer of Hebrews advises:

> Exercise foresight and be on the watch to look [after one another], to see that no one falls back from and fails to secure God's grace (His unmerited favor and spiritual blessing), in order that no root of resentment (rancor, bitterness, or hatred) shoots forth and causes trouble and bitter torment, and the many become contaminated and defiled by it.
>
> Hebrews 12:15 AMPC

According to this scripture, if resentment, hatred, or bitterness cause strife, many people will be contaminated and defiled by it. Regrettably, I have seen this to be true.

In the beginning of our ministry, more than forty years ago, God spoke to my heart three things we should do if we wanted to be blessed:

1. Always walk in integrity, which means to always do what we say we will do, always be honest with the money over which God makes us stewards, and always tell the truth.
2. To do whatever we do with excellence, to do as best we could, and to always go the extra mile.
3. Keep strife out of our marriage, family, and ministry.

We have made an effort to be obedient to God in these three areas. We have also taught them to our staff, and our ministry has indeed been blessed. When strife is allowed, it adversely affects God's anointing (grace and power), and that is something that we cannot do without if we want to enjoy God's presence and power.

Psalm 133 teaches us that where there is unity among people, there is also blessing and anointing.

If anyone who works for us stirs up strife and refuses to negotiate a peaceful resolution, we won't continue to employ them because I believe one person in strife can poison an entire ministry, church, or business if left unchecked. Strife includes gossip, critical judgment, and rebellion. As I mentioned at the beginning of this chapter, it will spread like a dangerous disease unless it is confronted.

Be a Strife Stopper

When strife comes our way, we can either feed it or stop it. We feed it by listening to it, agreeing with it, and perhaps adding to a story before we repeat it. Once we have told it, that person tells someone else, and the strife is like wildfire, spreading quickly and destroying everything in its path.

> When strife comes our way, we can either feed it or stop it.

If you have never seen this happen, you may think my assessment is excessive, but I know from experience that strife is indeed dangerous. In 2 Timothy 2:24, Paul writes that "the servant of the Lord must not strive" (KJV). The Amplified Classic translation says that a person who serves God "must not be quarrelsome (fighting and contending). Instead, he must be kindly to everyone and mild-tempered [preserving the bond of peace]."

In the preceding verse, he teaches us how to do that: "But refuse (shut your mind against, have nothing to do with) trifling (ill-informed, unedifying, stupid) controversies over ignorant questions, for you know that they foster strife and breed quarrels" (2 Timothy 2:23 AMPC).

It doesn't get much plainer than that.

When strife comes your way, instead of feeding it, stop it by simply telling the person that if they have a complaint against someone, they should go to that person privately and talk it out. In some cases, it is proper to tell them that every accusation should be confirmed by two or three reliable witnesses according to God's Word (Deuteronomy 19:15; 2 Corinthians 13:1) and that unless they provide witnesses, you will not believe the bad report.

A couple of years ago a woman called me and told me something bad about another woman, who happened to be a close friend of mine. I responded, "I don't believe that." She went on to tell me who told her and so on and so forth. I said, "I will call the person being accused and ask her if it is true."

I called and it was not true at all, but she did have a good explanation of how the rumor got started. I stopped the strife by calling back the woman who told me the story, letting her know it wasn't true and telling her to stop spreading it as though it was. I also asked her to call the people who had told her and let them know it wasn't true.

Why can't we fight *for* one another instead of against one another? Why are we so quick to spread a bad report about someone and so slow to tell something good, if at all? It is a ploy of Satan, because he knows we will have no power if he keeps us divided. He also knows that if we are united, he will be defeated.

> Why can't we fight for one another instead of against one another?

Strife exists today as I have never seen before, and people seem to delight in spreading it. Almost all news and social media outlets stay busy spreading bad news, which only feeds strife and makes situations worse. Let's make a commitment to not tell the bad things we hear unless someone truly needs to know them

and to make sure we repeat as much good news to as many people as we can. In this way, we can become strife-stoppers instead
of strife-spreaders.

Anything We Don't Feed Doesn't Live Very Long

Strife, like anything else, will die if it isn't fed. It can only survive
if people keep it alive by spreading it or feeding it by re-telling it
to others. Even weeds will die if they are not fed. Let me urge you
to be committed to not feeding strife. Treat others as you would
want them to treat you (Matthew 7:12), and walk in love as Jesus
instructs us to do (John 13:34). Remember that love is the highest calling on our lives. If what we do is not done in love, then we
should not do it.

In Genesis 13, we read that Abram (later

> Strife will die if it isn't fed.

re-named Abraham) knew this principle
well. For that reason, when strife arose
between his herdsmen and the herdsmen
of his nephew Lot, he went to Lot and said, "Let there be no strife,
I beg of you, between you and me, or between your herdsmen
and my herdsmen, for we are relatives" (Genesis 13:8 AMPC). They
were both so blessed that there wasn't enough fodder (grass) for
all the animals, so the men were fighting over the land. Abram
went to Lot, showing humility when he did, and told him to pick
the part of the Jordan Valley he wanted for himself and said that
he would take what was left (Genesis 13:9). This was indeed a
great display of humility because had it not been for Abram's generosity, Lot would have had nothing. Of course, Lot chose the
best part of the Jordan Valley for himself and Abram took the less
desirable portion.

But watch what happens next. God says to Abram:

"Look around from where you are, to the north and south, to the east and west. All the land that you see I will give to you and your offspring forever. I will make your offspring like the dust of the earth, so that if anyone could count the dust, then your offspring could be counted."

Genesis 13:14–16

Abram refused to feed the strife and it died. He chose to be a strife stopper, and God blessed him in amazing ways. The same can happen to you if you will starve strife instead of feeding it.

God wants to bless us, but we must get along with other people. Paul urges believers to be in perfect harmony and agreement, and to be united in their opinions and judgments (1 Corinthians 1:10). He also admonishes people to avoid strife by striving to keep unity and oneness with others (Ephesians 4:1–3).

> Abram chose to be a strife stopper, and God blessed him.

Satan hates agreement so much that he steadfastly fights against it. Since this is the case, we will have to fight just as hard in order to have it.

That They Might Be One

Jesus prayed a very special prayer in John 17. He prayed that we would all be one, just as He and the Father were one, so that the world would be convinced and believe that the Father had sent Him to earth:

Neither for these alone do I pray [it is not for their sake only that I make this request], but also for all those who will ever come to believe in (trust in, cling to, rely on)

Me through their word and teaching, that they all may be one, [just] as You, Father, are in Me and I in You, that they also may be one in Us, so that the world may believe and be convinced that You have sent Me.

John 17:20–21 AMPC

Just imagine how different the world would be today if we were all one as the Father, Son, and Holy Spirit are one. Our world is in serious trouble and one way to help heal it is for each one of us to be committed to keeping strife out of our lives.

When two people marry, God says the two individuals become one flesh: "A man leaves his father and mother and is united to his wife, and they become one flesh" (Genesis 2:24). Yet today, the divorce rate has skyrocketed among Christians and non-Christians alike. People live in strife and cannot seem to get along. But a large part of the reason for this is that they focus on their points of disagreement instead of the areas in which they do agree.

Everyone is hard to love some of the time, including you and me, but if we press past those times, we can have enjoyable, long-lasting relationships. You will never find anyone to have a relationship with who will please you all the time. All of us are imperfect, and in order to get along, we must be merciful and forgiving.

To be one doesn't mean that we are exactly alike, or that we think alike, have all the same opinions, and like all the same things. Oneness is based on a decision we make to find places of agreement and focus on them in our relationships. Of course, this requires humility and unselfishness. Are you willing to make oneness and unity a main goal in your life? Will you make the effort to live in unity for Christ's sake and for the glory of His Kingdom?

Thoughts and Strife

Our thoughts prepare us for action; therefore, the way we think about people has a great deal to do with how we get along with them. If we don't control our thoughts, they will drift in a direction that prepares us for strife. But if we purposefully think about people's good points, it will prepare us to deal kindly with the qualities we do not like about them.

> The way we think about people has a great deal to do with how we get along with them.

In terms of the five love languages, my husband is not a gift giver, but he is a man who does acts of service. I can choose to think a lot about the fact that he rarely buys me gifts and how it irritates me, or I can think about how blessed I am that he does the dishes at night, takes out the trash, and does most anything else I ask him to do that would be considered a menial task. He makes the bed each morning and fills my humidifier with water. He is very protective of me and always wants to make sure I don't get hurt. Last night I was carrying a couple of dishes down the steps, and he said, "Be sure you hold on to the banister. I don't want you to fall."

Dave is not one to discuss his deepest inner thoughts. He is more of a private person. For example, if he is sick, he might not ever tell me. If he does mention not feeling well, he does so after he feels better. I would prefer that he talk to me about everything, because that is the way I am with him. But he isn't that way, and if I want to enjoy oneness with him then I need to accept him as he is. He may not be a big talker, but he does take good care of himself. He wears the same size clothing he wore when we married in 1967, and he always looks his best. These are things that are important to me. So, he may not tell me all his deepest thoughts, but he does look good!

Nobody gets everything they want

> Nobody gets everything they want from a person.

from any one person, but we all get some things. So start looking for the aspects you like about each person in your life and you'll find living in harmony and agreement much easier.

CHAPTER 8

Love Is Not Easily Offended

Every day we have plenty of opportunities to get angry, stressed or offended. But what you're doing when you indulge these negative emotions is giving something outside yourself power over your happiness. You can choose to not let little things upset you.

Joel Osteen

Paul writes that love is not easily offended, nor is it "touchy" (1 Corinthians 13:5 AMPC). This is because love is not focused on itself. Anytime we are overly focused on how we feel, we are likely to find a reason to feel hurt, offended, angry, bitter, resentful, and a host of other negative emotions.

If we believe the best of people, rather than being suspicious of them, it will be much easier to not be easily offended. We can waste many days of our lives being offended and the person with whom we are offended may not even know how we feel nor realize they offended us. Love is not easily offended.

People who are easily offended are usually insecure, and they need to grow spiritually. Satan wants us offended. He wants division, but God wants love, peace, and unity. God loves everyone and wants us to be the same way. True love, the God kind of love, doesn't pick and choose who it loves, it just loves.

More than anything in my life, I want to please God and serve

Him during my time on earth, and I pray that you feel the same way. God doesn't exist simply to serve us and give us everything we want, but we exist to fellowship with, worship, and serve Him.

> God doesn't exist simply to serve us.

It is easy to see as we search and study God's Word that loving one another is the most important thing God wants us to do. But if we allow ourselves to become offended, peace is no longer possible and love grows cold.

There is a happy end for the person of peace (Psalm 37:37). Just think about it: Learning to resist conflict allows you to enjoy your life even if your circumstances are less than ideal. One way we can do that is by believing the best of people and not being easily offended.

Satan's Bait

Offense is called Satan's bait. The word *offense* comes from the Greek word *skandalon*. This describes the part of a trap on which bait hangs to lure its victim. Satan "roams around like a lion roaring [in fierce hunger], seeking someone to seize upon and devour" (1 Peter 5:8 AMPC), but it doesn't have to be you or me. If we are wise and learn to recognize and avoid the devil's tactics, we can walk in love and live in peace.

Offense is also a hindrance or a stumbling block. First Peter 2:6–8 says that Jesus is the stone over which people stumbled. They refused to believe and receive from Him, and that caused them to stumble in their spiritual lives.

In Mark 4:17 we learn that there are people who, although they believe in God, "have no real root in themselves, and so they endure for a little while; then when trouble or persecution arises on account of the Word, they immediately are offended (become displeased, indignant, resentful) and they stumble and fall away" (AMPC). These are weak believers, baby Christians who can only be happy and committed when life is easy and they are getting everything they want.

Everyone faces trouble, trials, and temptations, and we should not be offended when they come our way. Are you angry or offended with God because something you wanted has not happened, or because you have had to endure difficulty that you cannot understand?

Offense is one of the devil's favorite tools to use against God's people because he knows it keeps us in turmoil and prevents us from loving one another. The

> Offense is one of the devil's favorite tools.

Webster's 1828 Dictionary says this about the word *offend*: "To displease; to make angry; to affront. It expresses rather less than make angry, and without any modifying word, it is nearly synonymous with displease. We are offended by rudeness, incivility and harsh language. Children *offend* their parents by disobedience, and parents *offend* their children by unreasonable austerity [sternness] or restraint [restrictions]."

We are not to take offense or give offense, and we should make an effort to do neither. Don't take Satan's bait and be lured into his trap. Be wise and stay in love at all times. This is the best spiritual warfare you can wage. When we love, we are dangerous to the devil; when we don't, he is dangerous to us.

Matthew 24 lists signs of the end times, and one of them is that the "love of the great body of people [the Church] will grow cold because of the multiplied lawlessness and iniquity" (v. 12 AMPC). We definitely live in wicked and lawless times, and when we focus too much on the world's problems, I think it can make us cynical and distrusting. Instead of focusing on loving one another, we may look for the flaws in people, expecting them to hurt us. If we spend our time trying to protect ourselves, we cannot reach out and be inclusive of others.

Remember that Satan loves division, hatred, bitterness, resentment, offense, and unforgiveness. We should avoid these as we would the plague because they poison the soul and kill love and kindness.

> Satan loves division, hatred, and resentment.

The apostle Paul prays the following prayer for the Church:

> And this I pray, that your love may abound still more and more in knowledge and all discernment, that you may approve the things that are excellent, that you may be sincere and without offense till the day of Christ.
>
> Philippians 1:9–10 NKJV

Notice that Paul prays that we will be "without offense." It is important to keep our hearts clear of offense and other poisonous feelings because out of our hearts flow the issues of life (Proverbs 4:23). Just take one week and notice how many angry people you come in contact with or how many are offended by someone or something. A woman I know spent a week counting how often she had an opportunity to be offended, and came up with forty times. Because she had heard this teaching on avoiding strife, she was able to not take the bait of offense one time. It was eye-opening to her to realize how often Satan tried to steal her peace and prevent her from focusing on loving people.

Choose Wisdom above Emotion

We all have an abundance of feelings (emotions), and it is easy to follow them instead of doing what we know is right. Wise people do what is right no matter how they feel. I like to say that the wise do now what will give them the life they desire later. I recently wrote a book on Proverbs called *In Search of Wisdom*. As I studied to write that book, I was amazed at how often Solomon encourages people to walk in wisdom and avoid foolishness. I have learned that when I choose to do what is right when it feels wrong and hurts, I grow spiritually. Being the first one to apologize or say I am sorry may be difficult, but if it is the right thing to do, just do it and be blessed for your obedience to God.

People who love God and love His Word make an effort to let nothing offend them or make them stumble (Psalm 119:165). They know the power of a peaceful life, and they want to love everyone because this is what God wants us to do.

Some people simply assume that loving everyone is impossible, but if we see people from God's perspective, we realize that it *is* possible with God's help and some attitude changes on our part. What great thing have we done if we only love those who love us and are easy to love? But, if we love those who are hard to love, we show that God's power is greater than any obstacle.

Wise people obey God. They have a reverential fear and awe of Him, which prompts them to obey Him even when they don't feel like it. When someone hurts or offends us, it may seem unfair and unreasonable for God to expect us to forgive them and continue loving them, but if we trust God, we realize that all His ways are best for us. To me, nothing feels better than to be filled with love instead of ill feelings toward others. I don't like being angry or offended and have learned during my lifetime that it is wasted energy because it does nothing good.

Obeying God is wise because I believe the day is coming sooner than we think when every person will give an account of their life to Him (Romans 14:12). We won't be judged regarding our salvation because we cannot earn that, but we will be judged concerning what we have done or not done during our time on earth and rewarded accordingly.

I don't think nearly enough Christians pay attention to their actions. They attend church and call themselves Christians. They believe in God and have received Jesus as their Savior, but what are they doing? What are you doing? What am I doing? Are we doing what God wants us to do? The main thing He wants us to do is to love one another.

We should love one another as Jesus loves us.

Jesus gave us one new commandment: That we should love one another just as He loved us. By this love, He says, everyone will know that we are His disciples (John 13:34–35).

If we forget everything we have learned and focus only on love, we will not sin, because love does no harm to its neighbor (Romans 13:10).

The Wheat and the Weeds

In Matthew 13:24–30, Jesus tells a parable saying:

> The kingdom of heaven is like a man who sowed good seed in his field. But while everyone was sleeping, his enemy came and sowed weeds among the wheat, and went away. When the wheat sprouted and formed heads, then

the weeds also appeared. The owner's servants came to him and said, "Sir, didn't you sow good seed in your field? Where then did the weeds come from?" "An enemy did this," he replied. The servants asked him, "Do you want us to go and pull them up?" "No," he answered, because while you are pulling the weeds, you may uproot the wheat with them. Let both grow together until the harvest. At that time I will tell the harvesters: 'First collect the weeds and tie them in bundles to be burned; then gather the wheat and bring it into my barn.'"

In this parable, the wheat represents godly people and the weeds represent the ungodly. It teaches us that God allows godly people and wicked people to dwell together on earth in hopes that the godly will be obedient to Him and have a positive influence on the wicked. However, if the ungodly don't change, the time will come when they will be gathered and separated from those who are godly. The wicked will be destroyed, but the godly will live with God for eternity and enjoy the rewards of their obedience.

"The Son of Man will send out His angels, and they will gather out of His kingdom all things that offend...and all who practice evil" (Matthew 13:41 AMP). Now is the time for all of us to be making right decisions, to choose what is wise, and to be obedient to God's commands, especially those regarding love.

Offense and Cold Love

The apostle Peter writes that our love should be fervent and deep. Fervent means intense or hot and burning. When love is fervent, it will cover a multitude of sins (1 Peter 4:8). Look carefully at this scripture:

> If your enemy is hungry, give him food to eat; if he is thirsty, give him water to drink. In doing this, you will heap burning coals on his head, and the Lord will reward you.
>
> Proverbs 25:21–22

I used to think the burning coals mentioned in Proverbs 25:21–22 represented some kind of punishment our enemies would endure because they had mistreated us, but I learned the coals represent fervent love. When we heap burning coals on an enemy's head, we make them our friend. It is love that melts the hard heart of our enemies. Don't let your love grow cold, but keep it fervent and red-hot.

Put on Love

Paul teaches that more than anything else, believers should "put on love" (Colossians 3:14). What does this mean? How do we "put on" love? We put on love by purposely loving, rather than waiting to feel like doing it. I have never gone into my closet and stood there and had my clothes jump off the hanger onto my body. I have to carefully select what I want to wear each day. If I put it on and don't like the way it looks, I change my clothes until I do like them and think I look good in them.

We put on love by purposely loving.

We all look good in love, so let's put it on and keep it on. Take off attitudes that don't look good on you as a believer in Jesus Christ. The two words *put on* are used in several places in the Bible and they simply mean to do something on purpose. For example, we are to put on Jesus Christ (Galatians 3:27), put off the old self and put on the new self (Colossian 3:9–10, and put on our shoes of peace, breastplate of righteousness, helmet of salvation, and belt of truth (Ephesians 6:13–17). These comprise the uniform of a soldier of God, and they are the armor that protects us in spiritual battles.

To me, love is like an armor of light, and where love goes, light goes. We can spread light into the present darkness in the world by putting on love and walking in it. Only light dispels darkness; nothing else has the power to do it. I do believe we can have a positive influence on our society today and see it change for the better, but it will take each one of us doing our part consistently and not relenting because of pressure applied by evil people.

When the devil whispers in your ear, "That person is too hard to love," remind him that he is a liar and that all things are possible with God (John 8:44; Matthew 19:26). Never forget that love is not a feeling, but a decision about how we will treat a person.

Love is not touchy or easily offended. The moment you feel offense being offered to you, say "No, thank you." Stay in peace and walk in love, and you will have a life that is enjoyable.

CHAPTER 9

What Is Your Opinion?

Try being informed, not just opinionated!

Author Unknown

An *opinion* is defined as "a view or a judgment formed about something, not necessarily based on fact or knowledge" (lexico.com). Everyone has opinions. Some people are wise enough to keep theirs to themselves unless someone asks for them, but others feel compelled to offer their opinion on every subject that comes up and in every conversation.

I think it is interesting to note that an opinion represents what someone thinks and is not necessarily based on facts or real knowledge. So, what is an opinion really worth? There are as many opinions in the world as there are people, and I think placing too much value on the ones that come from a total lack of knowledge is unwise. A person's opinion may be right, but it may be wrong. You may consider it along with other input you receive, but be careful about letting other people's opinions run your life. Don't ever let anyone else's opinion become your reality, and don't let anyone else's opinion of you determine your sense of worth and value.

> Don't let anyone else's opinion become your reality.

"I Think"

How often do we say or hear others say "I think"? Quite frequently it seems. Why are we so interested in telling people what we think? Does it make us feel important to appear to know things? Is pride behind the frequent desire to give an opinion?

We live in a strife-filled world, and much of the strife arises because people offer their opinion and are then offended if others do not accept or adopt it. I readily agree that everyone has the right to have their own opinion, but does the fact that we have a right to have an opinion also mean that we have a right to give it? Just imagine how many arguments would be eliminated if we would simply keep our opinions to ourselves unless people request them. Even then, we should make sure that what we say as we articulate our perspective is based on knowledge or fact, not simply on what we think.

We have many thoughts about what other people should and shouldn't do, what they should own, and how they should manage their lives, when in reality we may not be doing a very good job running our own lives. Someone recently asked me what I thought they should do about a certain situation, and I told them I didn't think I was qualified to answer that question. I then suggested that the person ask someone else, someone I thought might be better qualified than I. There is no shame in simply saying "I don't know." It is better than pretending to know and giving wrong information that someone may follow and thereby cause trouble for themselves.

To put it plainly, if we want to enjoy peace, we need to learn to mind our own business.

Make it your ambition and definitely endeavor to live quietly and peacefully, to mind your own affairs, and to work with your hands, as we charged you.

1 Thessalonians 4:11 AMPC

We see from this scripture that minding our own business and living quietly and peacefully go together. We won't have one without the other.

Social Media

Although social media provides us with the ability to communicate quickly and is a source of information, it has also become one of the most dangerous forms of communication we use today. Many people use it as a place to spew out their disapproval of people and situations. It is a hotbed of "opinions." The real problem is that most people believe what they read without bothering to check its validity, and they are quick to spread what they have read to others.

Social media is a breeding ground for unfounded rumors, and it is often used to destroy a person's reputation. Anyone can say anything they want to say on social media. I have been the target of lies spread by the media, in which things I said were taken totally out of context, and there was nothing I could do about it except trust God to take charge of my reputation. Some people believed the lies and stopped supporting our ministry, but others said, "I don't believe that," and I am thankful for them.

One report said that I had died, and our ministry got lots of phone calls about that. Then I had to get on social media and tell people I was still alive. Another said I was selling weight loss pills, which is not true, and we had people calling the ministry trying to buy them and then being angry when told them we were not selling diet pills. Another rumor said that I was encouraging people to follow a certain diet program, and that is totally untrue. These are just a few samples of untrue statements that have been made about me, so I urge you not to believe everything you read or hear without checking it out thoroughly with reliable sources. Always be sure you check out your information before believing anything simply because someone said it.

> Do not believe everything you read or hear without checking it out thoroughly with reliable sources.

My dear friends, don't believe everything you hear. Carefully weigh and examine what people tell you. Not everyone who talks about God comes from God. There are a lot of lying preachers loose in the world.

1 John 4:1 MSG

The Bible teaches us not to gossip and be talebearers. Here are a few scriptures to consider the next time you are tempted to gossip or spread rumors.

Besides that, they learn to be idlers, going about from house to house, and not only idlers, but also gossips and busybodies, saying what they should not.

1 Timothy 5:13 ESV

With his mouth the godless man would destroy his neighbor, but by knowledge the righteous are delivered.

Proverbs 11:9 ESV

For lack of wood the fire goes out, and where there is no whisperer, quarreling ceases. As charcoal to hot embers

and wood to fire, so is a quarrelsome man for kindling
strife. The words of a whisperer are like delicious morsels;
they go down into the inner parts of the body.

                                    Proverbs 26:20–22 ESV

According to this last scripture, we can stop the spread of gossip and rumors by simply not passing them on. One of the dangerous aspects of mean-spirited gossip is that once we tell it to
someone, it taints their opinion of the person being talked about
even if they don't want to believe it. It goes down inside of them
and makes them a little suspicious.

And finally, a scripture that should make all of us think seriously about our own behavior:

> They were filled with all manner of unrighteousness, evil,
> covetousness, malice. They are full of envy, murder, strife,
> deceit, maliciousness. They are gossips, slanderers, haters
> of God, insolent, haughty, boastful, inventors of evil, dis-
> obedient to parents, foolish, faithless, heartless, ruthless.
> Though they know God's decree that those who practice
> such things deserve to die, they not only do them but give
> approval to those who practice them.
>
>   Romans 1:29–32 ESV

It's More Serious Than We Think

We often don't think much about making an unloving comment
about another person, but if we take seriously the scriptures we
have just read, it is apparent that speaking flippantly and unkindly
about another person is more serious than we think it is.

I would imagine that on a semi-regular basis, most people make comments that are not loving about people. In fact, their words may be critical and leave others with a less-than-stellar opinion of them. What if we only talked about people the way we'd like them to talk about us? If we did, a lot of our conversation about people would change.

We enjoy the mercy that God gives to us, and He expects us to show that mercy to others. Mercy is always greater in God's sight than judgment: "Mercy triumphs over judgment," James 2:13 says. God wants us to be patient and long-suffering with people, just as He is with us.

What is in our heart and mind eventually comes out of our mouth. If we think something long enough, we will end up saying it to someone else. This is why I say that loving people, even those who are hard to love, begins in the mind.

Passing Judgment

Once we form opinions, judgment is not far behind. In the same way that dread leads to fear, opinions can lead to judgment, and judging others in a critical manner has nothing to do with love. Paul writes, "You, therefore, have no excuse, you who pass judgment on someone else...So when you, a mere human being, pass judgment on them and yet do the same things, do you think you will escape God's judgment?" (Romans 2:1, 3).

Judgment belongs to God and one definition I read says that when we judge other people, we set ourselves up as God. Wow. I hope we all have enough reverential fear of God not to presume to do that.

We can judge sin, but we cannot judge a person's heart. Only

God knows enough about a person to do that. The more we study God's Word, the sooner we will recognize sin and bad behavior, and at this point in our walk with God we must be careful not to become prideful and set ourselves up as judge and jury when we see another person sin.

Sadly, many people judge and then share their opinion with others. In doing this, they open themselves up to an attack from the devil, due to their lack of love.

Instead of letting what we know make us prideful, we should let it make us more obedient.

We must also beware of forming quick judgments: "Therefore do not pronounce judgment before the time, before the Lord comes, who will bring to light the things now hidden in darkness and will disclose the purposes of the heart. Then each one will receive his commendation from God" (1 Corinthians 4:5 ESV).

There is a wonderful story in John 8:1–11 about a woman who was caught in adultery and the way Jesus handled her accusers. The scribes and Pharisees (the most religious men of their day) brought a woman who had been caught in adultery and placed her in the midst of a crowd. They said to Him, "Teacher, this woman has been caught in the act of adultery. Now in the Law, Moses commanded us to stone such women. So what do you say?" (John 8:4–5 ESV). They said this to test Jesus, hoping to find some kind of offense with which they could charge Him. He was teaching love, forgiveness, and mercy, and they were waiting to see if He would break God's law. Jesus bent down and wrote on the ground with His finger (John 8:6). Have you ever wondered what He was doing when He wrote on the ground? I have wondered, and I believe He was taking time to hear from His Father about how to handle this volatile situation.

As they continued to question Him, He stood and said to them,

"Let him who is without sin among you be the first to throw a stone at her" (John 8:7 ESV). He then bent down and continued to write on the ground. But when the accusers heard what Jesus said, the Bible tells us:

> They went away one by one, beginning with the older ones, and Jesus was left alone with the woman standing before him. Jesus stood up and said to her, "Woman, where are they? Has no one condemned you?" She said, "No one, Lord." And Jesus said, "Neither do I condemn you; go, and from now on sin no more."
>
> John 8:9–11 ESV

This story has many wonderful lessons in it. One of them is that *only* those who have no sin of their own have a right to judge another. It is important to take time to hear from God before answering a difficult question. Jesus did not condemn the woman, but He did tell her to go and sin no more.

> Only those without sin have the right to judge another.

People judge according to the flesh, but God sees the heart (1 Samuel 16:7). We quickly judge what we do not understand and have no experience with. We judge based on our carnal opinions or the lies that Satan tells us. But God is merciful, and He sees a person's heart. He knows what has happened to people to make them the way they are. He calls sin what it is and tells people not to sin, but He doesn't try to make them feel guilty and condemned when they do.

Let's use our imagination and consider some situations that might fit this subject. You or I might look at a possession someone has and "judge" that the person should not have spent money on such an item because we consider it wasteful. But, in reality someone gave them the item as a gift, or they received it as part of an inheritance. In that case, we would be judging something we knew nothing about.

We might see someone out shopping, making an expensive purchase, and we know that person is struggling financially. We judge that they should not be buying such a thing, when in reality, they are shopping for someone else as part of a second job they have taken in order to get out of debt. We should not assume we know what we do not know.

We need discernment, not opinions that are not based on truth. We love the following scripture when it is applied to us, but are we willing to apply it to other people? "But the Lord said to Samuel, 'Do not look on his appearance or on the height of his stature, because I have rejected him. For the Lord sees not as man sees: man looks on the outward appearance, but the Lord looks on the heart'" (1 Samuel 16:7 ESV).

David, a Man after God's Own Heart

The Bible tells us that David was a man after God's own heart (1 Samuel 13:14). How could God's Word say this, since David committed adultery with Bathsheba and had her husband killed to cover up the fact that Bathsheba was pregnant as a result of her time with David? Surely, most of us would have judged and condemned him and said he should have no longer been king.

Had social media been around in those days, I can just imagine how fast the rumors would have spread.

> There is a big difference between wickedness and weakness.

God was merciful to David because He knew his heart. There is a big difference between wickedness and weakness. David was not wicked, but he did have human weakness.

David thoroughly repented for his sin (Psalm 51), but he experienced consequences because of it. The child Bathsheba carried died (2 Samuel 12:18). God's prophet Nathan told David that the sword never would depart from his house (2 Samuel 12:10–11), and the story of David's life and family bears this out. Even so, David remained king. God loved David greatly—the man after His own heart (1 Samuel 13:14; Acts 13:22).

We are to judge fairly and righteously, not at a glance, superficially or by appearances (John 7:24 AMPC). We judge according to people's actions, but we cannot see what is in their heart. God looks on the hidden person of the heart and loves the beauty of a gentle and quiet spirit (1 Peter 3:4). He wants us to be more concerned with what is in our heart than with our outward appearance (1 Samuel 16:7). The Bible speaks of serving God with a whole heart (Psalm 9:1), a willing heart (2 Chronicles 29:31), a pure heart (Matthew 5:8), a contrite heart (Psalm 51:17), a new heart (Ezekiel 36:26), a clean heart (Psalm 51:10; Hebrews 10:22), a repentant heart (1 Kings 8:47–48), and a heart of compassion (Mark 6:34; Colossians 3:12). All I can say is, "God help me, because I cannot do it without You!" In our human strength, it seems too hard, but again, all things are possible with God (Matthew 19:26).

The Harvest of Judgment

All seeds that are planted bring some kind of harvest. If I plant weed seeds, I will get a weed harvest, and if I plant seeds of beautiful flowers, I will get a harvest of flowers. All of our words, thoughts, and actions are seeds we plant. Galatians 6:7–9 tells us that we reap what we sow. For example, if we are merciful, we will receive mercy (Matthew 5:7), but if we judge others, we will be judged (Matthew 7:1–2).

If we sow according to the harvest we would like to reap, the world would be a much better place. Make a decision and ask God to help you to stop judging people. Pray for them and leave the situation in His hands.

CHAPTER 10

Are You Angry with Yourself?

And, beloved, if our consciences (our hearts) do not accuse us [if they do not make us feel guilty and condemn us], we have confidence (complete assurance and boldness) before God.

1 John 3:21 AMPC

I believe a major reason so many people in the world are angry is that they have a guilty conscience. They are angry with themselves, and that anger comes out of them against other people. Some people today are like dysfunctional boilers ready to blow at any moment. If you work with the public, perhaps as a server or a store clerk, I am sure you have ample opportunity to witness just how angry people can become over minor situations that do not warrant the anger they display.

Even people who know nothing about the Bible and have no training as a Christian still know deep down inside when they are living in sin. They feel guilty, grouchy, and unhappy, but they may not be facing the reason for the negative ways they feel. God created us for holiness, not sin, and if our lives are filled with sin, we cannot be happy.

People who live in sin look for other people and things to make them happy, and when that doesn't happen, they feel and display anger. They have no peace or joy. I always go back to my father as an example of what a sinful life does to a person. He often made comments such as "I'm just as good as anybody else" and sounded as though he were defending himself when no one was accusing him of anything. He felt bad because deep down he knew his behavior was wretched. He was abusive, mean, and angry. He found fault with everyone except himself.

When he finally did give his life to Jesus, he became a different man. He was sweet and gentle, used no foul language, and stopped being critical of others.

God's Word teaches us not to do things that go against our conscience—things that we believe are wrong and do not have God's approval (Hebrews 10:22; 13:18). Many Christians miss out on the life Jesus died for them to live because even though they have received Him as their Savior, they have yet to make Him their Lord. They still think and act in ways they know are wrong, and believe me when I say that nothing is worse than having a guilty conscience. It is with you all the time. It will keep you from getting a good night's sleep and be with you the minute you wake up in the morning.

Deflecting

People with a guilty conscience often deflect their feelings by finding fault with others. As long as they can think about what someone else is doing wrong, real or imagined, it keeps them from having to deal with their own attitudes and actions.

> People with a guilty conscience often deflect their feelings by finding fault with others.

Another name for this type of behavior is blame shifting. Instead of taking responsibility for our own wrong behavior and doing what is necessary to make it right, we shift the blame to someone else. For years, I used the sexual abuse in my childhood as an excuse for everything I did wrong, especially when I was angry or irritable. I excused my own behavior and shifted the blame to someone or something else. I think we all tend to do that to a certain degree. Let's say a man says to his wife, "Everywhere we go, you are always late," but instead of saying, "You're right and I need to change," she blame shifts or deflects by saying "Well, if you would help me around the house when we are preparing to get out the door, then I wouldn't be late."

I did this with Dave for years. I already felt so bad about myself that if he tried to correct me about anything, I deflected it by finding some fault with him. When you are in a relationship with someone who is hard to love because they are often angry, you should remember that their anger probably comes from the way they feel about themself. Realizing this will help you know how to pray accurately for them. It is easier to deal with difficult situations if you understand them.

Is Jesus Your Savior and Your Lord?

To receive Jesus as our Savior is a benefit to us; to make Him Lord of our lives is something we do for Him. When He is Lord of our lives, we obey Him because we love Him and appreciate all He has done for us. This is one way we can say "Thank You that You have forgiven my sin and promised to be with me always."

Relating to Jesus as Lord is also beneficial to us because when we obey Him, we do not have a guilty conscience. In addition, obedience to God opens the door to many blessings in our lives. Lord is the name we use for Him more often than others, but it is more than just a name; it means that we have completely turned over our lives to Him and want His will more than we want our own. This does not mean that we don't make mistakes, but that our heart's desire is to do God's will in all things and that we receive His correction joyfully when it is needed. Ephesians 5:15 teaches us to be very careful how we live, and those who have made Jesus their Lord will do this.

I recently spent about thirty minutes with someone who is dealing with a divorce and some health issues. During the time we were together, he said at least four times, "I know I should" or "I know I shouldn't," and then he would tell me that he wasn't doing it. To know what is right to do and not do it is sin (James 4:17). The best course of action this man could take is to repent for his past disobedience and make a quality decision to begin following the guidance of the Holy Spirit and obey what God is leading him to do.

I don't think it is inaccurate to say that most people feel guilty about something. They know what they should or should not be doing, but they are not acting on that knowledge. The best way to live guilt-free is to do the right thing to begin with, or to at least admit your sin, repent, ask for God's forgiveness, and receive it. Repentance is not merely saying "I'm sorry I sinned," but changing your mind and changing your actions. It means turning from going your own way and going God's way.

> The best way to live guilt-free is to do the right thing to begin with.

Doing the right thing is much better than spending your life asking for forgiveness and trying to overcome the guilt connected with sin. When God forgives our sin, He also removes the guilt of it, but letting go of the guilt is often difficult for us. I wrestled with guilt for many years, even though I truly believed that God had forgiven me. Many people use guilt as a means of self-punishment even though Jesus took their punishment when He suffered and died for their sin (Hebrews 9:14; 10:17–18; 1 Peter 2:24). This is what I was doing without realizing it. Thankfully, I have been set free from that torment. Now, when I sin, I am able to receive forgiveness for the sin and let go of the guilt.

When Jesus is Lord of our lives, we live for Him. He is our life, and "in him we live and move and have our being" (Acts 17:28). He becomes everything, and we know that we are nothing without Him. Paul said, "I have been crucified with Christ and I no longer live, but Christ lives in me. The life I now live in the body, I live by faith in the Son of God, who loved me and gave himself for me" (Galatians 2:20).

Do Not Offend the Holy Spirit

The Holy Spirit lives inside of us as children of God, and He is often depicted as a dove, which represents gentleness. When Jesus was baptized by John, the Holy Spirit descended on Him in the form of a dove (Matthew 3:16). The Holy Spirit is our "Comforter (Counselor, Helper, Intercessor, Advocate, Strengthener, Standby")" (John 14:26 AMPC). He is our Teacher and our Guide, and He convicts of sin and convinces of righteousness (John 16:8). Because He is gentle, He doesn't like turmoil, and the world is filled with turmoil.

We are told not to grieve the Holy Spirit, which according to the Amplified Bible, Classic Edition translation means not to "offend or vex or sadden Him" (Ephesians 4:30). Perhaps sometimes when we feel sad, it is because we have saddened the Holy Spirit, and since He lives in us, we feel what He feels. Ephesians 4:30 goes on to say that we are "sealed (marked, branded as God's own, secured)" by the Holy Spirit "for the day of redemption (of

> We should live carefully, desiring at all times to please God.

final deliverance through Christ from evil and the consequences of sin)" (AMPC). This means we should live carefully, desiring at all times to please God.

People can grieve the Holy Spirit with "foul or polluting language," and with evil, unwholesome, or worthless talk (Ephesians 4:29 AMPC). When we think of all the complaining, gossip, criticism, and foul language in the world today, it is not difficult to understand why the Holy Spirit would be grieved. We cannot be responsible for what others do, but each of us can and should do our part to speak words filled with life.

Other things that grieve the Holy Spirit are bitterness, wrath, rage, bad temper, resentment, anger, quarreling, contention, slander, and malice, which is described as "spite, ill will, or baseness of any kind)" according to Ephesians 4:31 (AMPC). What pleases Him is walking in love. We are to be "useful and helpful and kind to one another, tenderhearted (compassionate, understanding, loving-hearted), forgiving one another [readily and freely], as God in Christ forgave" us (Ephesians 4:32 AMPC). It is obvious from these scriptures that mistreating other people for whom Christ died is offensive to the Holy Spirit. To think about grieving the Holy Spirit actually grieves me. I know I have done it many times, and I am sorry for each one. But just imagine how He feels, considering the condition of the world today. The world is so filled with hatred, anger, bitterness, unforgiveness, and turmoil that He surely must be greatly grieved.

As a reminder, my purpose in writing this book is to help us love everyone, even people who are hard to love, because God is love and He wants us to work with Him to "overcome evil with good" (Romans 12:21). We must set an example for the world because some people truly are like lost sheep without a shepherd.

As we have seen, love is much more than a word, and I strongly encourage you to study love intensely and deeply until you realize what it is and learn to make it your main goal in life.

The church is suffering intolerable defeat by the enemy due to a lack of love among her individual members. Putting on love is the most effective tool for defeating Satan.

> Putting on love is the most effective tool for defeating Satan.

Conscience and Confidence

A guilty conscience is a big problem for many reasons, one of which is that it blocks boldness and confidence. It hinders us in prayer. When we pray, we should pray boldly and with confidence. Jesus understands human nature because He lived on earth in a fleshly body and was tempted as we are, yet He never sinned, and He is always ready to forgive. But if we try to pray with a guilty conscience, our prayers are ineffective.

> For we do not have a high priest who is unable to empathize with our weaknesses, but we have one who has been tempted in every way, just as we are—yet he did not sin. Let us then approach God's throne of grace with confidence, so that we may receive mercy and find grace to help us in our time of need.
>
> Hebrews 4:15–16

God wants us to come before His throne boldly and with confidence and to pray, expecting to receive what we ask for. But we cannot do that with a guilty conscience.

If there is hidden sin in your heart, I urge you to go before

God and get everything out in the open, receive forgiveness, and refuse the guilt and condemnation that tries to hang on. God already knows everything we have done, so confessing our sins is for us, not for God. We feel better when we unload the burden of our sin.

> Confessing our sins is for us, not for God.

King David is an excellent example of what happens when we try to ignore our sin. David committed adultery with Bathsheba, and when they discovered she was pregnant, he had her husband, Uriah, killed in battle. David had a close relationship with God, but in a time of weakness, he did a terrible thing. A year passed before he finally confessed his sin and received forgiveness. In Psalm 32, he clearly tells us how miserable a person can be when trying to hide sin.

When I kept silent, my bones wasted away through my groaning all day long. For day and night your hand was heavy on me; my strength was sapped as in the heat of summer. Then I acknowledged my sin to you and did not cover up my iniquity. I said, "I will confess my transgressions to the Lord." And you forgave the guilt of my sin.

Psalm 32:3–5

Maintaining a Clean Conscience

Maintaining a clean conscience is very important, and we want to make sure we don't do anything that our conscience tells us is wrong. Paul said that his "conscience [enlightened and prompted] by the Holy Spirit" bore witness with him (Romans 9:1 AMPC). His conscience agreed with his actions. Conscience is a valuable function of our spirit. It condemns what is wrong and approves what is right. We should always work with the Holy Spirit to have a clean conscience. If I say something disrespectful to Dave, I immediately feel the conviction of the Holy Spirit, and I cannot get rid of the feeling until I apologize to God and to Dave. The moment I do, the guilt is removed.

The Holy Spirit is given to us to help us know when our actions are sinful, and we should be thankful for His ministry in our lives.

> Don't do anything that your conscience tells you is wrong.

There is such a thing as false guilt, and I suffered with it for many years. I felt guilty about things that God's Word does not disapprove of, but because my conscience was weak, Satan took advantage of me when I did them. Even if I enjoyed myself, I felt guilty about it. I had to learn the Word and the character of God before I could recognize when I was truly guilty of wrongdoing and when Satan was dumping false guilt on me merely to prevent me from enjoying my life.

I encourage you always to check everything against God's Word in order to know what truth really is. Paul teaches us that "Everything that does not come from faith is sin" (Romans 14:23). Our conscience should approve our actions. It may condemn certain actions we have taken, and we can justify our actions by making excuses for them, thereby relieving the pressure we feel from our conscience, but the Word of God states that when we do this, we are deceiving ourselves (James 1:22). Let us pray regularly for the Holy Spirit to guide us into all truth so that we are not deceived.

> Pray regularly for the Holy Spirit to guide you.

Paul shows us the importance of having a clean conscience when he writes that he always exercised and disciplined himself in order to have a "clear (unshaken, blameless) conscience, void of offense toward God and toward men" (Acts 24:16 AMPC). We will not and cannot keep a clean conscience unless we deal with sin by saying no to anything we know to be wrong.

If You Can't Do It in Faith, Don't Do It

We all have things we would like to do, yet when we do them, we have doubts or an uneasy conscience. Therefore, we should not do them.

I love good movies. When a movie begins in a wholesome way and then begins to include indecent scenes or foul language, turning it off can be difficult for me. I know I do not need to continue watching it, but I want to finish it so I will know how the story ends. However, I have learned that watching a movie with a guilty conscience is not worth doing in the long run. I know many people who are not convicted at all when watching movies that I feel condemned about watching, and I often wonder why. But God has taught me that each of us is responsible for being personally obedient to Him, no matter what anyone else does. Our place is not to judge anyone but to love them.

> Our place is not to judge anyone but to love them.

Daniel is a good example of a man who followed his conscience, no matter what he had to give up to do so. When he was taken into the king's court and ordered to eat rich food and drink wine, he felt he would defile himself because he had vowed to God that he would not eat certain foods. Even though he knew it could be dangerous to him, he went to the chief of the young men and asked to be able to eat only what he felt would be right for him. God gave him favor, and he received permission to follow his heart (Daniel 1:3–20).

Joseph is another example of someone who refused to compromise when pressured to do so. When Potiphar's wife wanted to have sex with him, he would not compromise for the sake of his conscience, even though he knew refusing her would mean going to prison. Joseph always did what he felt he could do in faith, and because of it, God gave him favor everywhere he went. He went to prison for making the godly choice with Potiphar's wife but ended up being promoted to the palace and being in charge of all the food during a famine. No one had more authority in Egypt than Joseph, except Pharaoh (Genesis 39–41).

One way we can tell if what we are doing is right is by whether or not we feel we need to hide it. If we are living a godly life, we can do so in the open light of day with no need to hide.

Deal Harshly with Sin

If we want to keep our conscience clear, we cannot be soft on sin. Jesus said that if your hand, foot, or eye cause you to stumble, it is better to throw them away (or cut them off) than to be thrown into hell (Matthew 18:8–9).

> We cannot be soft on sin.

Jesus said, "If your hand or your foot causes you to stumble, cut it off and throw it away. It is better for you to enter life maimed or crippled than to have two hands or two feet and be thrown into eternal fire. And if your eye causes you to stumble, gouge it out and throw it away. It is better for you to enter life with one eye than to have two eyes and be thrown into the fire of hell."

Matthew 18:8–9

When we sin, it is important to call sin what it is and not try to hide it under other labels, such as "my problem," "my weakness," or "my mistake." Sin is sin; it should be called what it is and confronted boldly. The writer of Hebrews says we are to "throw off everything that hinders and the sin that so easily entangles. And let us run with perseverance the race marked out for us" (Hebrews 12:1). These are strong words that teach us to deal harshly with sin.

Matthew wrote that the kingdom of God "suffers violent assault, and violent men seize it by force [as a precious prize]" (Matthew 11:12 AMP). We need to be aggressive and, at times, even violent against sin. I have lived with a guilty conscience, and I have lived with a clean conscience, and I can testify that living with a clean one is far better. It is worth anything we have to give up in order to have it. Nothing is better than peace in our hearts.

I believe many people are living with the heavy burden of guilt, and it makes them short tempered with others. God did not create us to feel bad about ourselves, and when we do, it does not have a positive effect on us. Work with the Holy Spirit to keep your conscience clean, and you will find it much easier to love people.

> Nothing is better than peace in our hearts.

Remember, if you don't love yourself, loving others will be impossible.

CHAPTER 11

Let It Go

To forgive is to set a prisoner free and discover that the prisoner was you.

Lewis B. Smedes, *Forgive and Forget:*
Healing the Hurts We Don't Deserve

There is no hope of loving people who are hard to love—in fact, no hope of loving anyone at all—unless we are willing to forgive and let go of their offenses. No one on this earth can have a relationship and never disappoint, hurt, or offend another. If you are hoping for this type of relationship, you will be looking for it all your life and not find it. Simply put, people are not perfect. If we were, we wouldn't need Jesus. He forgives us countless times, possibly every day, and we should appreciate what He does for us enough to do the same for other people. It is interesting that we want and even expect God to do for us what we are not willing to do for others.

In actuality, when we forgive people, we are doing ourselves—not the other person—a favor. So, do yourself a favor and forgive. Let go of offenses and the pain that accompanies them instead of carrying heavy burdens of unforgiveness that make you miserable. The Scriptures include many instructions to forgive people

> It is impossible to love people unless we are generous with forgiveness.

who have hurt us. Yet, I believe Satan gains more ground in most Christians' lives through unforgiveness than through any other means. We can hear the sermons, read the books, read the Bible, and believe wholeheartedly that we *should* forgive, yet still not do it. Why? We don't think it is fair, we don't know how to do it, or we don't understand that forgiveness is a process that isn't based on feelings. I will address these later in this chapter.

First, let me establish that it is impossible to love people unless we are willing to be generous with forgiveness. God loves us, and He forgives our sins. He forgets them completely and never mentions them again.

> The Lord your God is in the midst of you, a Mighty One, a Savior [Who saves]! He will rejoice over you with joy; He will rest [in silent satisfaction] and in His love He will be silent and make no mention [of past sins, or even recall them]; He will exult over you with singing.
>
> Zephaniah 3:17 AMPC

As human beings, even if we think we have forgiven an offense, we find it difficult to never mention it again. But according to 1 Corinthians 13:5, love "takes no account of the evil done to it" (AMPC). This means that love doesn't pay attention to or keep a record of how many offenses someone has committed.

I was once a great accountant of offenses. I could remember and remind Dave of things he did that made me angry years previously. Then, when we argued, I not only talked about what he did that made me angry in the present, but I also usually brought up situations from the past. I remember his asking me once, "Where do you keep all that stuff stored?" I could easily remember past offenses because I never totally forgave them.

Real love forgets how it has been hurt; it doesn't remember. It could remember if it wanted to, but love realizes that carrying those unpleasant memories is a waste of time and energy.

The Lord's Prayer teaches us to pray, "Forgive us our debts, as we also have forgiven our debtors" (Matthew 6:12). I seriously doubt that we really want God to forgive us as we forgive others, because we are not always good at extending forgiveness to those who have hurt us. But if we do not forgive the sins of others, neither does our Father forgive ours (Matthew 6:15).

I wonder how many people miss out on a close relationship with God because of the unforgiveness they carry in their heart toward other people. Unforgiveness negatively affects our prayers, our worship, and our fellowship with God, as well as our relationships with those we are angry with.

It Isn't an Option

God's Word commands us to forgive. It isn't an option. God's Word says we *must* forgive: "Bearing with one another and, if one has a complaint against another, forgiving each other; as the Lord has forgiven you, so you also must forgive" (Colossians 3:13 ESV).

We can, of course, choose not to obey in the area of forgiveness, but we pay a price for doing so. We hurt ourselves more than we hurt other people by refusing to forgive. Refusing to forgive is like taking poison and hoping our enemy will die.

> We hurt ourselves more than we hurt other people by refusing to forgive.

We may spend years being angry with someone who doesn't know or care that we are angry. They are living their life and enjoying it, while we are miserable and bitter.

If we want our prayers to be answered, forgiving people's sins is something we will have to do. God's Word teaches us that when we pray, if we have anything against anyone, we must forgive the person and let it go, so that our heavenly Father may forgive us (Mark 11:25). Many people cannot understand why their prayers are not answered, but they never search their heart to make sure it is clear of offense toward others. Perhaps we should search our heart before we pray. This way, if we have anything against anyone, we can forgive them and then present our requests to God.

I don't want anything to hinder my relationship with the Lord, because it is the most important relationship I have. Sin of any kind can hinder it, and unforgiveness is a sin.

It's Not Fair

One of the first objections that often comes to mind when we consider forgiving someone who hurt us is that it isn't fair. My father abused me sexually for years and years. He was mean, violent, and controlling. He created an atmosphere of fear that made everyone in the family miserable, but God required me to forgive him. When I realized this, my first thought was *It's not fair.* He was not sorry for what he had done, yet I was being asked to forgive him. I carried a burden of hatred and resentment toward him in my heart until I was in my forties. Even then, when I did forgive him, at first it wasn't complete forgiveness. One truth that really helped me was learning that hurting people hurt people. Once I realized this, I saw that my father had something wrong inside of him that made him the way he was.

Jesus prayed on the cross for His crucifiers to be forgiven, saying they didn't know what they were doing (Luke 23:34). When people hurt God's children, He will be our Vindicator and will repay the offenses against us if we let them go and leave them to Him to deal with. He is a God of justice, and in due time, He will make right everything that is wrong.

Forgiveness is the beginning of healing for the wounded soul and the brokenhearted person. The genocide that took place in Rwanda in 1994 included one hundred days of slaughter in which eight hundred thousand people were violently murdered. More than a million were killed before the war was stopped. This was one of the most horrific events in history, and it involved violence that is almost unimaginable. I visited Rwanda years after the massacre and had the privilege of speaking with some of the victims about the importance of forgiveness. I watched as many of them released the burdens they had carried, and I saw the change that took place in them. I told them it was okay to let go of the past and go on with their lives. Previously, they had thought that letting go would be disrespectful to those who had died, but they saw the truth of God's Word and finally began to live again.

Eighty-five percent of the Rwandan people were from the Hutu tribe, but the minority tribe, the Tutsis, had always been in control. In 1959, the Hutus took control and thousands of Tutsis fled to neighboring countries. In a well-organized plan, the Hutus arranged for the slaughter of the Tutsis. According to BBC.com, "Neighbors killed neighbors, and husbands even killed their Tutsi wives." The slaughter was so massive that the bones of the victims have remained piled high in the country for years. They have worked to forgive, and much progress has been made, although I am sure there is still a great deal to be done. There is no hope of things such as this being forgiven without God's grace to help.

I have read countless stories of people who have forgiven what would seem to be unforgiveable offenses. Here are a few of them:

The Unlikely Pardoner

Iranian woman Samereh Alinejad had told The Associated Press that "retribution had been her only thought" after her teenage son was murdered. But in a dramatic turn at the gallows, literally moments before the killer was to be executed, Alinejad made a last-minute decision to pardon the man. She is now considered a hero.

The Understanding Widower

After a long shift at the fire department, Matt Swatzell fell asleep while driving and crashed into another vehicle, taking the life of pregnant mother June Fitzgerald and injuring her 19-month-old daughter. According to *Today*, Fitzgerald's husband, a full-time pastor, asked for the man's diminished sentence—and began meeting with Swatzell for coffee and conversation. Many years later, the two men remain close. "You forgive as you've been forgiven," Fitzgerald told *Today*.

The Compassionate Officer

According to an excerpt of the book *Why Forgive?* in *Plough Quarterly*, Steven McDonald was a young police officer in 1986 when he was shot by a teenager in New York's Central Park, an incident that left him paralyzed. "I forgave [the shooter] because I believe the only thing worse than receiving a bullet in my spine would have been to nurture revenge in my heart," McDonald wrote. While the younger man was serving his prison sentence,

McDonald corresponded with him, hoping that one day the two could work together to demonstrate forgiveness and nonviolence. Unfortunately, the young man died in a motorcycle accident three days after his release. [McDonald died in 2017, but he spent the rest of his life traveling the country and spreading the message of forgiveness.]

None of these events would have been considered to be fair. But don't forget what Steven McDonald said: "The only thing worse than receiving a bullet in my spine would have been to nurture revenge in my heart."

It may appear that these people did something amazing for the ones who hurt them. While this may be true, they actually did more for themselves. They let themselves out of prison.

Understanding the Process of Forgiveness

Just as love is not based on feelings, but is a decision about how we treat an individual, so is forgiveness. We forgive because God tells us to forgive. He never tells us to do anything unless it is best for us, and He never tells us to do something that is impossible for us to do. Even though forgiving may be difficult, we can trust that doing so is wise because God says to do it.

> God never tells us to do anything unless it is best for us.

When we decide to forgive someone who has hurt us, we probably won't feel any differently toward that person initially. Most people make the mistake of thinking that if their feelings do not change, they have not forgiven. I hope to bring some understanding to the process we can expect to go through when choosing to forgive someone, because assuming we have not forgiven because our feelings have not changed simply is not true.

1. Choose to obey God.

First, we decide to obey God and forgive. This begins with a prayer asking God to help us forgive the person who hurt us. We declare that we forgive that individual, and we make a commitment to pray for them. God tells us to pray for our enemies and those who persecute us (Matthew 5:44).

How should we pray? What do we pray for? Pray for people to be forgiven for what they have done to you and ask God to bless them with understanding about how their actions affected you. In addition, ask Him to help them understand how their actions affect themselves, so they can see the truth and ask His forgiveness personally. When we ask God to bless to our enemies, He may not give them a new car or a promotion at work, but He will bless them with truth that will set them free. However, if they do receive some kind of materialistic blessing, we should resist the urge to be jealous and think they don't deserve it. It is the kindness of God that leads people to repentance (Romans 2:4).

It is very difficult to continue hating someone you are praying for regularly. Pray that God will give you an understanding heart toward your enemy. When people mistreat others, there is always a reason for the way they act. More often than not, they were mistreated themselves and are simply acting out what is in their soul.

2. Don't speak negatively.

The next step in the process of forgiveness is to make a commitment not to speak ill of the person who hurt, offended, or wronged you. You may be tempted to tell others what the person did or how they treated you, and you may have talked about it previously, but once you choose to forgive, it is important to also choose to refrain from negative comments about them.

3. Help.

Finally, be prepared to help them if they need help. The Bible says, "If your enemy is hungry, feed him; if he is thirsty, give him something to drink" (Romans 12:20). In other words, if your enemy has a need and you can meet it, then do so. Nothing softens a hard heart more quickly than giving to someone who has hurt you.

This process of forgiveness is what helped me to forgive my father and mother for their abuse and abandonment, and it is ultimately what led my father to repent of his sins and receive Christ as his Savior. My sacrifice was very small compared to the joy of knowing that he is in heaven now and that we will have the joy of a perfectly loving relationship when I get there.

I have stated that forgiveness is not a feeling, but it's important to add that your feelings eventually will catch up with your decision to forgive. However, you may never feel about the person the way you would have if they had not hurt you. My mother asked me thirty or forty years after I left home how I felt about her, and I was truthful. I told her that I didn't love her as I would have loved a mother who protected me and took care of me, but that I did love her as a child of God and would always make sure she was well cared for.

We rely far too much on our feelings to tell us the truth, but they can easily deceive us. We should not give our feelings the power that we often allow them to have over us. I don't imagine

> We rely far too much on our feelings to tell us the truth.

Jesus felt like going to the cross, but He did. We don't know how He felt when He was being rejected, spat upon, abandoned, and betrayed, but I doubt He felt good about it. Nonetheless, He did obey His Father in heaven, regardless of how He felt.

Answer these few questions in order to honestly evaluate your position toward forgiveness.

- Do you have anything against anyone at this time?
- Do you make your decisions about love and forgiveness based on your feelings?
- Do you pray for your enemies?
- Do you speak negatively to others about those who have hurt you?
- Are you willing to help your enemies when they have a need?

This chapter may present an opportunity for new beginnings for you. In fact, it could change your life. I urge you to work through the process of forgiving anyone who has hurt you and to be willing to do it over and over again. Don't put limits on what you will do for others, because God does not limit His mercy and forgiveness toward us, and He will give you the grace and strength to obey His teaching to forgive, knowing that it will set you free.

PART 3

The Power of Love and Acceptance

CHAPTER 12

Can't You Be More Like Me?

The older I get, the more I believe the greatest kindness is acceptance.

Christina Baker Kline, *A Piece of the World*

In order to love people, we must learn to accept them as they are, not try to make them the way we wish they were. In many cases, we expect people to change themselves and be more like we are before we are willing to give them the acceptance they desperately need. When I speak about accepting people the way they are, I am not talking about accepting sin and giving people the idea that we think everything they do or think is okay. I am talking about not trying to change people into something or someone other than who God made them to be. This is vitally important for healthy relationships.

People living in sin know they are sinning, and our pointing it out to them or judging them for it won't make them change. Only love and prayer will be used by God to change the heart of a difficult person. Trying to force them to change is useless, because only God can work in a person's heart and bring the changes He knows are needed.

> Only love and prayer will change the heart of a difficult person.

Unconditional Acceptance

Dave and I didn't date long before we married. We certainly didn't allow enough time to really get to know each other. You might say that our marriage was more of a divine connection. We had only five dates before Dave asked me to marry him. He was praying about finding the right girl to marry, asking God to give him someone who needed help. And he certainly got his prayer answered, because I was as dysfunctional as anyone could be. But I didn't know I had problems.

I didn't even know what love was, but I said yes to his proposal, and off we went into our adventure called marriage. It didn't take very long, probably not even a week, before I began to notice things I didn't like about Dave. I wanted him to spend our entire one-week honeymoon hanging curtains in our apartment, and I could tell he didn't really want to do that, and it aggravated me. In those days, I had such a deep root of rejection that if anyone even slightly acted as though they didn't want to do something I asked them to do, I felt rejected. However, at the time I didn't know what I was feeling. All I knew was that I felt hurt. The hurt turned into anger and then came pouting and self-pity. I was a champion pouter! I gave Dave the silent treatment sometimes for days and even weeks at a time because he wasn't making me feel the way I wanted to feel.

I gave Dave the job of keeping me happy, and for a while he tried, but he soon discovered I wasn't going to be happy no matter what he did. So, one day he simply told me he was tired of trying to keep me happy and that he intended to be happy and enjoy his life, whether I enjoyed mine or not.

You can imagine how this infuriated me, but it turned out to be one of the best things he could have done. He did not allow me to control him, and although that angered me, I did spend less time being angry because I realized I wasn't achieving the result I desired: getting my way. Dave didn't try to change me. He loved me as much as I would let him. I can definitely say that I received unconditional acceptance from Dave.

I Thought Dave Needed to Change

Dave didn't try to change me, but I tried to change him. I was sure that my way was right in every situation. I tried to talk him into changing, I tried to guilt him into changing, I tried and tried, but nothing changed. I got angry, I gave him the silent treatment, and I pouted. He played a lot of sports, and I wasn't interested in any of them, so I wanted him to give them up and stay home and help me or pay attention to me. Everything was about *me*.

I know I sound like I was a terrible person, and my behavior was terrible, but I honestly didn't know any better. I was repeating what I had seen growing up. My father was extremely controlling, and unless the world revolved around him, he made everyone in the family miserable. I truly believed the reason for my bad behavior was that other people did not do what I thought they should have done. I thought that if they would only change, I could be happy. I wanted everyone to change except me. It took me years to finally learn that people cannot change other people; only God can truly change a person. True change must come from the inside out, not from the outside in. As Paul writes in Romans 12:2, we are to be *transformed*, not conformed. God transforms us into the image of Jesus Christ, but the world and the people in it want us to conform to what they want us to be.

> I believed the reason for my bad behavior was that other people did not do what I thought they should have done.

When I say that Dave gave me unconditional acceptance, I don't mean he never confronted me about my behavior. But he confronted me infrequently and only when he believed God was leading him to do so. Mostly, he prayed for me and trusted God to change me.

When we try to change people, we send messages of rejection, not acceptance. God has designed us for love and acceptance, and nothing works in relationships except giving people the gifts of love and acceptance. God loves and accepts us. He takes us the way we are and helps us get to where we need to be, but He does it with gentleness, kindness, and patience. God has changed me over the years, and I now recognize that I was the one with the problems and realize that my judgment of others blinded me to my own faults.

Dave needed to be changed in certain ways also, but only God could do that, and He has. Neither of us has been perfected, nor will we be until Jesus takes us to heaven. But we now know that we cannot change each other, and we have learned to pray and leave the changing to God.

If you are dealing with someone who is hard to love and that person is abusive or dangerous, then you will have to love them from a distance and continue praying. But don't give up on them. I cannot even imagine how awful my life would have been had Dave given up on me.

Who Are You Trying to Change?

Is there anyone in your life that you are trying to change, perhaps one of your children, a spouse, a parent, an in-law, a boss, a coworker, or a friend? I can save you a lot of grief if you will simply believe me when I say it won't work. Sometimes, if we complain enough, people will change for a while, but unless God changes their heart, they will revert to who they are inside.

The best plan, the one that is godly, is to pray about changes you think God needs to make in other people and do so with all humility, just in case you are wrong about them. Then work with the Holy Spirit to become the person God wants *you* to be and give unconditional love and acceptance to everyone else.

For a long time, I tried to change almost everyone with whom I had any kind of relationship, and my children were not exempt from my efforts. Have you ever noticed that no matter how many children you have, they are all different, and each one has their own method of frustrating you? I had one full-blown type A, one sanguine, one melancholy perfectionist, and one "I don't care about school, how my room looks, what kind of grades I get, or much of anything else" person. Of course, I worked on each of them, and I was well on my way to making them hate me when God finally got my attention and I learned that He makes all of us different and wants us to accept and value one another. What a boring world we would live in if we were all exactly alike. I was really bad about looking at what was wrong with people and not seeing all that was right about them.

> We try to make everyone else like us when we often don't even like ourselves.

Because we are deceived and often think we are perfect, we try to make everyone like us when we often don't even like ourselves. If we were successful in conforming others to our image, we wouldn't be able to find anyone we liked. God's plan is beautiful once we see it. We all have strengths and weaknesses, and as we learn to work together, we all do our part and become a body working together with Christ as our head (1 Corinthians 12:27).

Dave and I eventually learned that if we covered each other's weaknesses and put our strengths together, we had everything we needed to be successful at whatever we did. As far as my children are concerned, I laugh now when I think of how hard I tried to change them and didn't realize that they were just what I needed for the future. Our two sons run the day-to-day operations of our ministry, which reaches around the globe, and it is a huge job. One of our daughters is in ministry herself, and the other daughter (the "I don't care about anything" one) is my assistant, and I really don't know what I would do without her. She hated school and barely made it through, and now, by God's grace, she is super smart in all the areas in which she needs to be. I urge you to pray for your children, asking that they will be all *God* wants them to be, not all *you* want them to be. If you will do that, everything will turn out fine.

Trying to change other people is hard labor and very frustrating because it never works, so why not enjoy the aspects that you can enjoy in people and leave the rest to God?

Turn Yourself Over to God

Most of us, when we begin understanding God's Word, see what He wants us to be like and quickly realize we are a long way from that ideal. The next thing we tend to do is the worst thing we can do: We try to change ourselves, and that is God's job. God sent His Holy Spirit to live in us to teach us truth (John 16:13; 2 Timothy 1:14) and to convict us of sin and convince us of righteousness (meaning, the right way to behave; John 16:8). The Holy Spirit is our strengthener (Ephesians 3:16) and intercessor (Romans 8:26). When we receive Christ, we are sanctified and made holy, but the Holy Spirit takes the seed that God placed in us and develops it into full-blown fruit over a period of time

(Galatians 5:22–23; Ephesians 5:9). God puts holiness in us, and the Holy Spirit works it out of us, with our cooperation (Romans 15:16; 1 Peter 1:2).

Please read the following passage of Scripture slowly and grasp what it is saying. We work out what God has put in, but not in our own strength. We do it only with God's help.

> Therefore, my dear ones, as you have always obeyed [my suggestions], so now, not only [with the enthusiasm you would show] in my presence but much more because I am absent, work out (cultivate, carry out to the goal, and fully complete) your own salvation with reverence and awe and trembling (self-distrust, with serious caution, tenderness of conscience, watchfulness against temptation, timidly shrinking from whatever might offend God and discredit the name of Christ). [Not in your own strength] for it is God Who is all the while effectually at work in you [energizing and creating in you the power and desire], both to will and to work for His good pleasure and satisfaction and delight.
>
> Philippians 2:12–13 AMPC

Change takes time, and sometimes it takes a lot of time. I want to encourage you to enjoy yourself while you are changing. God does! He loves you and enjoys you at every stage of your spiritual growth. Just as we love our children at every stage of their growth, even though some stages are harder than others, we should love and enjoy ourselves through every stage of becoming more Christlike.

Yesterday we ate at a really nice restaurant with our son, his wife, and our four youngest grandchildren, ranging in age from eighteen months to thirteen years. The eighteen-month-old, Brody, has found his voice, but doesn't know the difference between his inside voice and his outside voice, so he often screams. He loves, loves, loves french fries, and yesterday two of his brothers had french fries. For a long time, Brody didn't see them. But when he did, he screamed, *"Fries!"* Rather than being upset because he screamed in such a nice restaurant, we thought it was funny, and so did the people around us.

We get too uptight about our faults and lose our joy over things that God knows will change in time. Obviously, over time Brody will be taught not to scream when he wants french fries, and

> We lose our joy over things that God knows will change in time.

God will also correct our faults. But just as our family members are enjoying the baby in his imperfect state, God enjoys us in our imperfect state and invites us to enjoy ourselves as well.

Let me encourage you to turn yourself over to God. Tell Him that you know you cannot change yourself, but that you want Him to change you and make you what He wants you to be. He will do it at a pace that is just right for you, and He will use methods that would not have occurred to you. It is God's grace that changes us, not our self-effort. All we can do is want to be what God wants us to be, repent that we are not, and put ourselves completely in His hands to make the changes that need to be made. Of course, we make an effort, but it is an effort made while depending on God, not ourselves, for victory.

God has changed me dramatically. I barely recognize myself when I think of the twenty-three-year-old girl who married after five dates and spent her honeymoon being angry with her husband because he didn't want to hang curtains.

How did God change me? He used His Word, specific books He put into my hands or led me to purchase, various teachings, time spent with Him, mistakes that taught me valuable lessons, and many other things that are still a mystery to me. He loved me even in my imperfect state, and that is what He asks us to do for others. Once I was blind, but now I see, as the song "Amazing Grace" says. God will change you too. The transformation of a human being is possibly the greatest miracle we witness in our walk with God. I will give you one piece of advice that I feel is very important: Never give up!

The Gift of Freedom

Freedom is one of God's greatest gifts. He gives us choices and tells us which ones will work out best for us, but He never forces us to make the ones He suggests. He sets before us "life and death, blessings and curses," and we get to choose between the two (Deuteronomy 30:19).

> Freedom is one of God's greatest gifts.

The best thing that Dave did for me was to set me free to be myself. He didn't allow me to be disrespectful to him, and he didn't let me control him, but he did and still does let me be myself. Even when I scream for...well, not for french fries, but scream nonetheless about something I want or don't want, he laughs at me because he knows my heart. He often says, "There's that old fire that I married you for." He was dating three girls when he met me, but he said they were all boring compared to me, and he wanted a challenge. Believe me when I say he got one!

God created Dave and me for each other. Dave accepts me the way I am, and I accept him. We are both still changing. In fact, just today I saw a miracle. I love to have my feet rubbed, and Dave doesn't love or even like to rub feet, so I stopped asking him to rub my feet years ago. But this morning as I was sitting and writing this book, he came over to where I was and started rubbing my feet—and then he even kissed one of them. I asked him if Jesus was coming back today and he was doing good deeds just to make sure he got to the right place (☺). Let me add that he didn't rub my feet for long, but he did rub them, and I have learned to be thankful for small beginnings (Zechariah 4:10).

On most days, there are countless situations about which we could both become angry if we wanted to, but we prefer to let love cover a multitude of sins (1 Peter 4:8). Love is so much more fun than arguing and anger, and it never fails in its effort to unite rather than divide. Trying to change other people is an act of self-ishness, not love.

Love is liberating. It offers people both roots and wings. It provides a sense of belonging and acceptance (roots) and a sense of freedom (wings). Love doesn't try to control or manipulate, and it doesn't seek its own fulfillment through trying to control the destiny of others. In a truly loving family, a father who dreamed of being a pro football player doesn't try to force his son to play football when he would rather be a dancer. A mother who wants her daughter to be popular because she never was doesn't force her to be a cheerleader, get in with all the "right" people, be on the debate team, or run for school president when she is more of an academic who wants to quietly study and isn't concerned about her reputation with people. Parents don't project certain roles onto their children because they accept and enjoy them as God made them to be.

> Love offers people both roots and wings.

Love finds out what people need and helps them get it.

CHAPTER 13

Please Accept Me!

To the praise of the glory of His grace, by which He made us accepted in the Beloved.

Ephesians 1:6 NKJV

God has promised never to reject anyone who comes to Him. Our behavior may not make us acceptable, but God makes us acceptable "in the Beloved," meaning in Jesus Christ. Because of our faith in Jesus, we are considered to be "in Christ," and since Jesus is acceptable to God, God views us as acceptable too.

Being accepted by God is wonderful, but we also crave acceptance from people. Everyone wants to be accepted, included, loved, and approved of, but not everyone around us is willing to give us these positive experiences. We must learn to deal with rejection, or we will be miserable much of the time. Jesus was rejected by the people He came to help, by religious leaders, and even by His own brothers who did not believe Him (Luke 9:22; John 7:5; Acts 4:10–11). He was hated "without a cause" (John 15:25 NKJV), and He said that if people hated Him, they will also hate us because a servant is not greater than his master (John 15:18–20).

We worry far too much about what other people think of us. Our real concern should be that God approves of us and our actions. The fact that people reject us doesn't mean something is wrong with us. They may have personal problems and find it difficult to approve of anyone because they don't approve of who they are or of something about their life. If they are critical and judgmental toward themselves, those negative feelings will flow out of them toward others.

Most people who mistreat other people have been mistreated themselves. How we feel about ourselves is more important than most of us realize. Do you accept yourself? Or do you reject yourself? Are you waiting to be more perfect in your behavior before you will accept yourself? Remember that Jesus died for us while we were still sinners (Romans 5:8). I'll say it again: You can enjoy yourself while God is changing you and making you more and more like Jesus.

> Most people who mistreat others have been mistreated themselves.

One of the Best Gifts

Acceptance is a gift we can give people, and it is a gift everyone wants. It isn't difficult to show; simply smiling at a person can be a sign of acceptance. A few words of affirmation or a quick compliment also does wonders for most of us. Let's purpose to help people feel accepted, keeping in mind that God accepts us in spite of our imperfections.

Other ways to help people feel accepted include being quick to forgive, showing mercy, and being patient with people when they make mistakes. Yesterday a young girl waited on us at a restaurant. We could easily tell that she was a new employee because she was nervous. She forgot to order Dave's sandwich, so while the rest of us were eating our meals, he only had soup. When she realized she forgot to order the sandwich, her face grew flushed, and we could tell it made her feel terrible. When she did bring it, Dave made sure he told her what a good job she did and let her know that forgetting the sandwich wasn't a problem at all. He told her we all make mistakes and not to worry about it. Interactions such as these are gifts we can give people that will help them in major ways.

Many people would become angry if someone forgot a major part of their meal. If a server is already insecure, anger spewed at them further damages their soul (mind, will, and emotions). Two of my granddaughters work at a fast-food restaurant. They recently told me that a woman spit on a server because she felt her salad wasn't made correctly. Another woman saw that her order wasn't correct and threatened to run over the server who delivered the food to her car. The servers are cursed at, threatened, and treated shamefully over tiny mistakes. How much better it would be if people could show mercy and be quick to forgive, but chances are they can't give mercy and forgiveness to others because they don't have these traits in them. Angry people are probably hurting themselves, and when others make a mistake, it is easy to take their frustrations out on them.

Many people in the world are hurting, and their souls are in pain for many reasons. Chief among them are past rejections that have left them feeling flawed and unacceptable. No doctor can prescribe a medication for that kind of pain, but God has enabled us to let Him work through us to be healers of the soul.

It is God's love and acceptance that heals us, but He often uses other people to pour out His love to us. One of the major ways God healed my wounded soul was through Dave's unconditional love and complete acceptance of me. Ask God to use you to show His love and acceptance to others. It will be one of the best gifts you can ever give anyone.

We tend to reject people who are hard to love, who are different than we are, who we don't understand, or who disagree with us. This isn't right, and it is time to choose to be a healer of wounds instead of someone who wounds others or makes their current wounds deeper.

Since God wants us to love everyone, we need to learn to look beyond our differences and see the value that is in people because God has created them and loves them. Let's learn to discern what is really going on when people behave badly instead of merely reacting to their behavior with our own bad behavior.

God loves every person on the planet and is especially kind to those who have been treated unjustly and are hurting. He loves them unconditionally, whether they love Him or not. Even if they don't agree with Him, He still loves them, and as His representatives on the earth, He wants us to do the same. Loving someone does not mean that we agree with all their actions, but it does mean we are kind and loving toward them.

> Loving someone does not mean that we agree with all their actions.

Our Differences

The world is filled with hatred, and much of it is based on differences between people. Some people hate those who are of a different race, a different culture, a different political party, or a different religion. Hatred started in Genesis and rears its ugly head throughout the Bible. Cain hated Abel and killed him (Genesis 4:8). Jacob disliked Esau, his twin brother, and cheated him out of his birthright, and Esau hated him for it (Genesis 27:1–29, 41). Joseph's brothers hated him because his father loved him more than he loved them, so they sold him into slavery but pretended that a wild animal had killed him (Genesis 37:4, 11–33). David's brother, Eliab, treated him with disrespect, and David's son, Absalom, tried to take the throne away from him (1 Samuel 17:28; 2 Samuel 15). The religious leaders of Jesus' day hated Him and the prophets He sent (Matthew 23:34; John 15:25). The people Paul had ministered to deserted him at his first trial, but he asked God not to hold it against them (2 Timothy 4:16).

History tells us of many so-called religious wars. Eight crusades were fought between the Christians and Muslims from 1096 until 1291 over control of holy sites that both groups considered sacred. Millions of people died during those crusades. The Thirty Years' War was a religious war that took place between Catholics and Protestants from 1618 to 1648. The persecution and execution of millions of Jews by Hitler and his followers during World War II is an example of how twisted a person's thinking can become when it is filled with hatred.

Sadly, a great deal of judgment exists between different Christian denominations and their ways of worship. For example, the Protestant may strongly disagree with the Catholic, or the Baptist with the Pentecostal, or the Pentecostal with the Lutheran or the Methodist. The list is never ending. Everyone thinks they are the only one who is right, but I have come to doubt that any of us is one hundred percent right. We may all be surprised when we get to heaven. We may even be surprised about who makes it into heaven and who doesn't. Each person should be convinced in their own heart about

> No one is ever one hundred percent right.

what they believe and avoid judging others. Sincere love would solve all these problems if we would simply let it.

There have been very few years in all of history when a war was not being fought somewhere. The statistics vary, so I won't offer a lot of numbers, but just as an example, one report I read said there had only been 268 scattered years without war (defining *war* as a conflict in which one thousand or more lives were lost) during the last 3,400 years in our world. Getting along with one another doesn't seem to be something people do easily, but it must be possible, because God instructs us to do it (Psalm 34:14; Romans 12:18; Hebrews 12:14). We can love one another even though we are different.

Many people reject others just because those people have a different personality than they do. This is all extremely foolish, because God is the one who made us different. John Ortberg wrote a book titled *I'd Like You More If You Were More Like Me*, and I love the title and the book. I wish I had thought of it before he did! The title of the book is a sermon in itself and presents a truth that we all deal with. We want people to be like we are, but God has made us all different on purpose so we can help one another. No one has everything.

We read in the Bible that Jacob loved a woman named Rachel and worked seven years for her father, Laban, to win her hand in marriage. But she had an older sister named Leah, and since it was customary for the older sister to marry first, Laban tricked Jacob into marrying Leah. Jacob did get to marry Rachel, but he did have to work for Laban another seven years for her (Genesis 29:16–30).

I find this story very interesting. Jacob loved Rachel. She was beautiful, but she was unable to have children for many years. Leah gave Jacob many children, but Genesis 29:17 says she had "weak eyes." I think this is a nice way of saying she wasn't pretty. Rachel had the beauty, but Leah had the children. I use this as an example when teaching on how everybody gets something, but nobody gets everything. If we understand this, we can stop being jealous of other people and learn to enjoy the gifts we have and the gifts they have.

Loving from a Distance

Paul encourages the Philippians to complete his joy by getting along with one another (Philippians 2:2). He also writes concerning two women named Euodia and Syntyche, and instructs the church to help them get along (Philippians 4:2–3). Yet even Paul had a sharp disagreement with Barnabas, during which they parted company and after which they no longer ministered together (Acts 15:36–41). However, after some time they learned to respect one another and spoke kindly of each other. It seems they continued to walk in love even though they disagreed in certain ways.

We know they disagreed about taking John Mark with them on their ministry journey. Paul felt he could not depend on him, but Barnabas felt differently, and he wanted John Mark to accompany them. Paul and Barnabas could not come to an agreement, so they went their separate ways. We might say that Paul and Barnabas loved one another from a distance. They couldn't work closely together, but still loved one another. We also see that Paul and John Mark later reunited and ministered together (2 Timothy 4:11; Philemon 24).

These are great examples for us to consider because they show that we can disagree agreeably. Even if we have trouble in certain relationships, it can be repaired, and we can come back together.

I have encountered situations like this. I remember two people I truly did love, but after years of trying to work together, I finally concluded that our personalities were too different for us to work closely together. We have remained friends and have supported one another in ministry, but we have not tried to work together. I do believe we can love someone and still not enjoy being around them a lot. Don't forget that love is not necessarily having loving feelings, but a decision to treat people as God instructs us to treat them.

When you read about loving everyone unconditionally, you may feel there are certain people you simply cannot love because of how they have hurt you or because they may still be abusive, and being around them would not be safe for you. You can love everyone, but that doesn't necessarily mean you need to spend time in their presence. Pray for people, don't speak unkindly about them, and help them if they need help, but always remember that you have a right to safe relationships.

Realizing that I can love from a distance has been extremely helpful to me. I once felt, as you may feel, that loving someone meant I had to spend time with them, but it doesn't. There were many years when being around my father wasn't safe or emotionally healthy for me, but as an adult, I still prayed for him and helped him and my mother financially when they needed it.

Remember: Love is how we treat someone, not how we feel about them.

> Love is how we treat someone, not how we feel about them.

Love Doesn't Enable Unhealthy Habits

Let me say a bit more about loving people while also maintaining healthy boundaries for yourself. A woman may be married to a man who is addicted to drugs and alcohol or who is abusive. He may have affairs with other women. Continuing to love that man doesn't mean she must continue living with him. Love doesn't always mean restoration of a relationship. Even though reconciliation may eventually happen, it may take a great deal of time. Sometimes something has to die before it can be resurrected. I know people who have divorced and years later remarried because the problem that forced them to separate has been corrected.

You can love a child who is a drug addict, but that doesn't mean you must or even should continue to enable their problem by rescuing them over and over again or letting them take advantage of you. It isn't good for them for you to do so.

Because of my mother's guilt about what she let my father do to me, she showered what she thought was love on my brother. He had a problem with drugs, especially prescription pain pills, and she often gave him money, knowing he would use it to support his addiction. She even let him have her medicine when he begged her for it. This kind of behavior is not real love. It simply enables an addict to perpetuate their problems.

If you have a child who is in their thirties, still living at home, not working, and struggling with an addiction of some kind, you may show more love by forcing them to get out on their own and take care of themself instead of taking care of them yourself. Tell them that you love them and always will, and that you will pray for them. Let them know that if they have a legitimate need that doesn't involve supporting their addiction, you will try your best to help them. But you don't have to let someone ruin your life because they have decided to ruin theirs. You can accept a person without accepting their behavior.

> You don't have to let someone ruin your life because they have decided to ruin theirs.

In 1 Timothy 1:19–20 we read that Paul handed Hymenaeus and Alexander over to Satan because they were teaching false doctrine and refused to be corrected. He didn't literally give them to Satan, but he did excommunicate them from the church for two reasons.

First, he needed to protect the church members from deception. Second, he hoped that getting put out of the church would cause them to realize their error and repent. You might say that Paul loved them from a distance. We often call this type of behavior tough love. In other words, we are showing love but in ways different from how people often think of love. It often requires more love to discipline a person you care about than to let them do as they please.

CHAPTER 14

Adapt and Adjust Yourself to Other People

Live in harmony with one another; do not be haughty (snobbish, high-minded, exclusive), but readily adjust yourself to [people, things] and give yourselves to humble tasks. Never overestimate yourself or be wise in your own conceits.

Romans 12:16 AMPC

I must admit that when I first read Romans 12:16, I was in no way prepared to adjust myself to other people. I wanted everyone to adapt to me. I felt this way especially toward Dave. He and I were very different in our temperaments and felt differently about many things, but we love one another and have learned to disagree while remaining in peace.

One area I can remember disagreeing about was how to discipline our children. For example, because I had been abused as a child, I rarely agreed with how Dave wanted to discipline them. I wanted to correct them without making them angry with me, and he didn't care how angry or unhappy they were as long as he felt he was doing the right thing and the correction worked. He was never mean to our children, but because my view of discipline was so skewed by being disciplined unfairly and violently as a child, I viewed totally appropriate and reasonable correction as unreasonable. People who have been abused usually have a dysfunctional perception of what is right and wrong. Dave and I disagreed in many other ways, often because of the way I was raised.

Dysfunction Breeds Dysfunction

Our role models serve as examples for us and teach us how to behave. Even if we don't like the way they treated us, we frequently end up emulating their behavior. My father always corrected me angrily and unfairly, so I viewed most correction as angry and unfair.

If you have been abused in any way, especially during your formative years, I encourage you to consider that the abuse may color your views on many things. If you find yourself frequently in conflict with others over the way things should be done, it is wise to study the Bible in that area or to listen to people who have wisdom and experience in it.

In our early years of marriage, Dave and I didn't argue all the time about everything, but when we did disagree, I usually persisted in trying to get my way. Because Dave was and is a peace lover and has an adaptable temperament, he often gave me what I wanted simply to keep the peace and because it didn't matter to him that much. Although this may be wise on some occasions, if it becomes out of balance it contributes to a problem rather than solving it. Dave did eventually begin to confront me, and between Dave and the Holy Spirit, I have learned how to adapt and adjust to other people instead of insisting that I always get my way.

In the Disney movie *Frozen*, the characters sing a song called "Let It Go." I often hear that song in my head when Dave and I don't agree. Petty matters are not worth arguing over. We now have a good balance. He gets his way in things that are really important to him and I get my way in things that are really important to me.

Adapting to Things

The amplification of Romans 12:16 says to adjust to people and things, so let's think about how we adjust to things. Consider a circumstance you don't like but cannot do anything about. How do you respond to it? Do you continue trying to change it to no avail, or do you trust God to take care of it and remain peaceful?

We all face circumstances we don't like. Over the past two weeks, the main furnace in our house went out and had to be replaced, but the company doing the repair couldn't get a new one for two weeks.

The weather was cold in St. Louis, where I live, so it was cold in the main rooms of the house. Thankfully, our bedroom and bathroom are on a different unit, but the kitchen, living room, family room, and lower level of our house were affected. I did not like it! I really don't like being cold—or hot for that matter. I guess I just don't like being uncomfortable.

At first, the situation frustrated me, and I felt angry toward the company for not keeping replacement parts in their inventory, but I quickly realized the circumstances would not adjust to me, so I needed to adjust my attitude toward them. The solution was that I bought a heater, used my fireplace, and found other ways to stay warm. These adjustments made me comfortable enough to do what I needed to do in the rooms that were so cold.

Being willing to adapt and adjust to what we cannot change is the only way to enjoy a peaceful life. Jesus says that each day

> Being willing to adapt is the only way to enjoy a peaceful life.

brings "enough trouble of its own," and for that reason, we should live one day at a time and not worry about tomorrow (Matthew 6:34). God gives us enough grace (power and ability) to handle life one day at a time and enough grace to handle the inconveniences or troubles of each day, but He will not give us tomorrow's grace today.

We often hear "Life is not fair," and it isn't, but God will bring justice if we patiently trust and wait on Him. In reading Paul's letters, I have noticed that he never prayed for people not to have problems or for their problems to go away. He prayed that they would have "the power to endure whatever comes, with good temper" (Colossians 3:12 AMPC). I am always amazed when I read, think about, or teach on this scripture. Our prayers are quite different than Paul's. We simply want our discomfort to go away, but Paul wanted something much more valuable. He wanted the people to be able to adapt and remain peaceful in the midst of their trouble. He knew this would make them stronger to handle future difficulties.

Do we always pray for the easy way out? I think we usually do, but we can learn from Paul's teachings and begin praying to be able to endure whatever comes with patience and good temper. Paul states in Philippians 4:12–13 that we can be content whether we are in need or have plenty, and that we can do all things through Christ who is our strength, whatever condition we are in. Let each of us ask ourselves if we are able to do this and answer truthfully.

I am at the point where I usually initially respond with aggravation but can adjust fairly quickly, realizing that if I cannot change something, I may as well not lose my joy over it.

Adapting to People

My first encounter with Romans 12:16, about adjusting to people and things, came when I was a young Christian trying to learn not to get upset when I didn't get my way. Adapting to Dave's way of wanting to handle a situation was very difficult for me. I struggled because I had a strong, selfish personality and because I had been mistreated by men and couldn't believe Dave would consider what would be best for both of us in making his decisions.

I eventually learned that peace is more valuable than getting my way, and I have grown in my ability to adapt to other people. I now see that adapting

> Peace is more valuable than getting your way.

and adjusting is one way we can show our love for God and people. I do stand up for myself if I feel I should, but I don't always have to have my way to be happy.

The apostle Paul seemed to be a master at adjusting to others. He writes:

> To the Jews I became like a Jew, to win the Jews. To those under the law I became like one under the law (though I myself am not under the law), so as to win those under the law. To those not having the law I became like one not having the law (though I am not free from God's law but am under Christ's law), so as to win those not having the law. To the weak I became weak, to win the weak. I have become all things to all people so that by all possible means I might save some.
>
> 1 Corinthians 9:20–22

The fact that Paul adapted himself to whatever would win the other person is a powerful principle that we should all study and learn to emulate. He was talking about winning them to Christ, but we can also apply these scriptures to simply being able to walk in love and maintain unity and peace. As previously stated, we don't adapt to sin, but we can humbly adapt to people who are different than we are. Notice I said "humbly," because being able to do it does require humility.

Living as Paul lived requires self-sacrifice, and I think we can say with all certainty that loving people and keeping the bond of unity is important enough to do whatever we need to do in order to obey God in this area. This doesn't mean that we must always do as others want us to do, but we simply cannot be the one who is right all the time and still maintain peace and unity. We cannot maintain good relationships with others if we are never willing to adapt to their desires or ways of doing things. It is probably safe to say that most divorces and losses of other relationships stem from selfishness and unwillingness to adapt.

Once we understand that adapting is giving, and that giving is a big part of walking in love, it becomes easier to do. At least it does if we are committed to walking in love, because love is the greatest thing in the world and the one new command that Jesus gives us (John 13:34–35).

Treat Everyone as Christ Would Treat Them

Treating everyone as Christ would treat them is a tall order, and I will admit that although it should be our goal, it isn't easy to do. We will need to slow down and ask ourselves, "What would Jesus do in this situation" if we ever hope to do it. We are accustomed to reacting to external stimuli, and instead of that, we need to train ourselves to act according to God's Word.

> We need to slow down and ask ourselves, "What would Jesus do?"

The Bible says we are to treat others as we would want them to treat us (Matthew 7:12). Of course, this would solve all relationship problems, but actually doing it is a challenge. We readily agree in principle that it is the godly thing to do, and we may even plan to do it. Yet when the time comes, often we are dealing with negative emotions that move us to action in a situation before we take time to consider what we would want done to us or what Jesus would do.

However, both of these goals are within reach, because God never instructs us to do anything we cannot do. We may not be able to do them without His help, but all things are possible with God (Matthew 19:26). If we mastered being able to live this way, there could be times when some people would take advantage of us, but we can't be so afraid of being taken advantage of that we won't do God's will. He will guide us concerning when to say no to someone for their own good.

I'm sure that if I always treat others the way I want to be treated, I will sacrifice a lot, because I frequently want others to sacrifice for me. Jesus not only sacrificed in situations He encountered, but He was Himself a sacrifice to God (Ephesians 5:2). He came to sacrifice His entire life for us that we might be saved. Paul writes that we should offer our bodies as living sacrifices (Romans 12:1). Let me encourage you to begin each day by asking God what you can do for Him that day before asking Him for everything you want Him to do for you. If we ask Him how we can serve Him, He will show us many ways, and they will usually require some kind of sacrifice.

Busyness

We are busy people, and our busyness often prevents us from serving others. However, Jesus always took time to stop and help others and meet their needs. He was always going somewhere, and He rarely made a trip without being stopped by someone who wanted Him to heal them or help a friend or relative.

In Luke 10:25–37, Jesus told a parable about a good Samaritan and some so-called religious people who encountered a man lying the side of the road. He had been beaten and robbed, and he desperately needed help. A priest and a Levite both saw the man and crossed the road to avoid having to walk past him. I often wonder if they were on their way to church, or perhaps they were just busy.

The Samaritan, who was also on his way somewhere, stopped, tended to the man's wounds, and then took him to a place to receive proper care. He needed to keep going on his journey, but he said he would pay all the expenses for the injured man's care when he returned, and he didn't even put a limit on how much he was willing to spend. Jesus asked which of these men had shown himself to be a true neighbor to the injured man, and the expert in the law said, "The one who had mercy on him," and then Jesus said, "Go and do likewise" (Luke 10:37).

The Samaritans were half Jewish and half Gentile, and the Jews and Samaritans had nothing to do with one another in that culture. The Samaritans did not follow Judaism as it was taught; they believed their own version of the first five books of the law and followed their unique version of worship. Nevertheless, the Samaritan showed love to the man in need, while the priest and the Levite—both Jews, who were God's chosen people—did not.

Being a Christian does not guarantee that a person will act in godly ways, but it should. We need to always do what we say we believe. We should be as Paul writes, living letters or epistles of Christ, "known and read by everyone" (2 Corinthians 3:2–3).

An Honest Evaluation

If you were to ask yourself if you are an adaptable person, what would your answer be? You may not be where you want to be, but you are doing well if you are making some kind of progress. As for me, I certainly have not arrived at the place of perfection, but I have made a lot of progress, and I adapt to others much more easily than I once did. I will keep pressing on, and I believe you will also. Remember, adapting is a way of showing love and maintaining unity and the bond of peace.

> Adapting is a way of showing love.

CHAPTER 15

We Are All Created Equal in God's Eyes

I have also decided to stick with love...hate is too great a burden to bear.

Martin Luther King Jr., "Where Do We Go from Here?"

In "Letter from a Birmingham Jail," Martin Luther King Jr. said, "Injustice anywhere is a threat to justice everywhere." The only way to overcome injustice and inequality is to learn how to love as Jesus loves. Throughout the ages, various races and cultures have fought against one another, just as we see in the world today. What we are experiencing today is nothing new; it's just happening among different groups of people in some cases.

In Jesus' day, the Jews hated the Gentiles, which meant that they had a lot of people to hate, because a Gentile was anyone of a non-Jewish nation or group. The Jews thought they were better than anyone else because they were God's chosen people. God's aim in choosing them was not so they would be prideful and think they were superior to other people; He chose to work through them with the goal of spreading the gospel to everyone.

When Jesus came to earth, He settled class distinctions once and for all. The apostle Paul writes, "There is neither Jew nor Gentile, neither slave nor free, nor is there male and female, for you are all one in Christ Jesus" (Galatians 3:28).

The entire human race is God's creation. In Acts 17:25–28, we see that God made all races and nations, all of us "from one blood" (v. 26 NKJV) for His purposes. God created each of us. We didn't choose which part of the world we would be born in, our race, or our skin color.

> The entire human race is God's creation.

Jesus was not a white man, as He is often shown in pictures. Based on where He was born, He probably had brown eyes, dark brown or black hair, and olive-brown skin. When He came to earth, He did not play favorites. The apostle Peter made a point of saying that "God is no respecter of persons" (Acts 10:34 KJV). He loves everyone and everyone who comes to Him will be treated equally. The promises of God are made to "whosoever will" (Revelation 22:17 KJV), or "whoever" will in more contemporary Bible translations, meaning that His promises are available to anyone who calls on Him.

God's Universal Call to Whoever Will

The gospel call has always been the same from Adam and Eve after they sinned, to Abraham, to Moses, to Malachi, to you and me, and to everyone else who ever lives.

"The heavens so declare the glory of God, and proclaim his wisdom, power, and goodness, that all ungodly men are left without excuse."

"Whosoever Will May Come,"
BibleTruths.org

Here are some of the scriptures that refer to whoever will:

> Whoever calls on the name of the Lord shall be saved.
>
> Romans 10:13 NKJV

> Whoever confesses that Jesus is the Son of God, God abides in him, and he in God.
>
> 1 John 4:15 NKJV

> For God so loved the world that He gave His only begotten Son, that whoever believes in Him should not perish but have everlasting life.
>
> John 3:16 NKJV

> Jesus said to her, "I am the resurrection and the life. He who believes in Me, though he may die, he shall live. And whoever lives and believes in Me shall never die. Do you believe this?"
>
> John 11:25–26 NKJV

Each of us fits into the category of "whoever." This means we all have equal opportunity for salvation and a personal relationship with God through Christ. And we all have equal opportunity to go to heaven. It's our choice.

The Racial Divide

The racial divide we deal with today is not new. I am not an expert on wars, but I know that many wars have been waged over the issue of race. These include, but are not limited to the various battles between colonists/US troops and Native Americans over an extended period of time, multiple wars in the Middle East, and wars between different tribes in Africa, including the Rwandan genocide mentioned in an earlier chapter. Perhaps one of the best-known wars based on race was World War II. During this conflict Adolf Hitler of Germany hated the Jews and managed to kill six million of them.

In addition, slavery throughout the world has been a terrible injustice, and we know that it was the key divisive issue in the American Civil War. Approximately 750,000 men died in that war. I wish we could go back and undo all that was done, but since it is impossible, I hope we can find a way to go forward that doesn't involve hatred, resentment, division, and violence. If we do it God's way—the way of love—we can find peace and new beginnings.

If we would take time to study these wars, we would see that war never solves our problems. Hatred cannot destroy hatred, and evil cannot destroy evil. Only love can conquer evil, and only good can overcome evil.

> Only love can conquer evil.

Peace and Love Can Lead to Victory

Martin Luther King Jr. believed that only love could heal the racial divide. Mahatma Gandhi, a leader who eventually succeeded in setting India free from British rule, believed that only love could overcome hatred. He said, "The weak can never forgive. Forgiveness is the attribute of the strong." He also said, "In a gentle way, you can shake the world." Both Martin Luther King Jr. and Mahatma Gandhi fought injustice, yet neither of them did so with violence. They believed that love conquers all.

Nelson Mandela was another great man, and he brought peace to a racially torn South Africa. Thomas Ashe said about him: "Mandela's name is synonymous to forgiveness, he will be remembered to have lived and died, loving and forgiving. Mandela said that 'Forgiveness liberates the soul, it removes fear.'" He was instrumental in bringing peace to South Africa. He fought for equality and an end to apartheid and shared the Nobel Peace Prize with Frederik Willem de Klerk in 1993.

Can You Broaden Your Circle of Inclusion?

Who do you include and who do you exclude in your life? We tend to exclude people who are not like we are, but those are the very people Jesus would have us reach out to. In the Old Testament, God told the Israelites to love the foreigner and stranger among them (Leviticus 19:34; Deuteronomy 10:19), and in the New Testament we are urged, "Offer hospitality to one another without grumbling" (1 Peter 4:9).

In our society, we are moving further and further away from one another, and I don't think this is good. In America today, we can live next door to someone for ten years and not know their name. We tend to isolate ourselves, and social media has made this worse, because we can send messages and images to people without ever seeing them.

A great deal of communication consists of body language and voice tones, not mere words. I have read that some experts say that 73–90 percent of communication is nonverbal. I think that, when possible, we should speak with others face-to-face. However, if it isn't possible, social media and texting are good options, especially for quick messages such as "Looking forward to lunch today," or "Sorry, but I will be five minutes late." Social media is also effective for answering questions people ask on social media platforms, as long as the answer is not too long or complicated.

Social media and text messaging are not good venues to try to convince someone of something or to bring correction.

Let me encourage you to try being friendly with all kinds of people. Just a hello or a smile conveys acceptance, which is something we all crave. I will admit that in the past I have tended to avoid people who were extremely different from me. I was in a coffee shop once, and the girl at the counter had three colors in her hair and piercings everywhere a person could have them. She also had ample tattoos. Without even thinking about what I was doing, I looked for another server. Someone who was with me that day went up to the girl and said, "I love your hair. How do you do that?" My friend struck up a conversation with her, and I realized that I was wrong in avoiding her. That wasn't what Jesus would have done.

> Try being friendly with all kinds of people.

Jesus Loves Everyone

When Jesus walked the earth, He showed love to everyone. And the apostle Peter writes, "God does not show favoritism but accepts from every nation the one who fears him and does what is right" (Acts 10:34–35). Jesus was available to everyone who believed in Him.

The Jews and Gentiles hated one another, but Jesus broke down the dividing wall between them: "For he himself is our peace, who has made the two groups one and has destroyed the barrier, the dividing wall of hostility" (Ephesians 2:14). Jesus can do the same for us today if we will let Him. He can destroy the barrier between two people, two nations, or two races. He came to earth to bring peace.

James 2:8–9 teaches us that love does not show favoritism: "If you really keep the royal law found in Scripture, 'Love your neighbor as yourself,' you are doing right. But if you show favoritism, you sin and are convicted by the law as lawbreakers."

James also encourages us to treat everyone equally by telling us not to treat a rich person better than a poor one:

> My brothers and sisters, believers in our glorious Lord Jesus Christ must not show favoritism. Suppose a man comes into your meeting wearing a gold ring and fine clothes, and a poor man in filthy old clothes also comes in. If you show special attention to the man wearing fine clothes and say, "Here's a good seat for you," but say to the poor man, "You stand there" or "Sit on the floor by my feet," have you not discriminated among yourselves and become judges with evil thoughts?
>
> James 2:1–4

God does not have favorites; we are all His favorite. We are all special to Him, and He is especially fond of each of us. No matter who you are, you are precious in His sight.

Loving everyone is demanding. It requires us to do some things we may not be comfortable doing, but we should widen our circle of inclusion.

> We should widen our circle of inclusion.

You Can't Love God and Hate People

First John 4:20 tells us that if we say we love God but hate our brothers and sisters in Christ, we are liars, because we cannot love God and not love His people. In this verse, John asks how we can love God, who we have not seen, if we cannot love those we do see.

I learned a long time ago that God does not take it kindly when we mistreat people. It is not a light matter, nor is it insignificant to God. Jesus came to earth, lived, and died for people, and we are His greatest interest. Each of us has multiple opportunities to help everyone we come in contact with feel better and we need to remember that. Would you take the challenge to try to make everyone you contact on any given day feel more valuable after you leave their presence than when you arrived? This can be done with a simple compliment or even a smile and a thank-you.

Jesus makes special mention of the poor, widows, orphans, the oppressed, and the lonely. We should take extra care to be kind to people in these situations. The Bible includes many wonderful scriptures about how to treat the poor, such as "He who oppresses the poor reproaches his Maker, but he who honors Him has mercy on the needy" (Proverbs 14:31 NKJV). If we help the poor, God promises to help us in our "times of trouble" (Psalm 41:1).

We need to treat everyone as well as possible. If you employ other people, it is important to treat them properly. Pay them well and show respect to each one. We all have closer relationships with some people than with others. Even Jesus appeared to be closer to Peter, James, and John, and of those three, John seems to have had a special place in Jesus' heart. In fact, John called himself "the disciple whom Jesus loved" (John 21:7).

We should not treat others in ways that make them feel devalued or unimportant. I think it is important to go out of your way to show appreciation to those people who may often be taken for granted—people who work in the nursery at church, people who clean the office where you work, and people who have seemingly unimportant jobs that are essential for everything else to work properly.

> Do not take advantage of a hired worker who is poor
> and needy, whether that worker is a fellow Israelite or a

foreigner residing in one of your towns. Pay them their wages each day before sunset, because they are poor and are counting on it. Otherwise they may cry to the Lord against you, and you will be guilty of sin.

Deuteronomy 24:14–15

> God wants people to help those who don't have as much.

God wants people who have more than others to use some of what they have to help those who don't have as much. He also wants us to do all we can to help them feel valuable and loved.

In the story of the good Samaritan (Luke 10:30–35), two Jewish men (a priest and a Levite) saw a man beaten and lying on the side of the road, and they crossed to the other side of the road to avoid helping him.

Then, a Samaritan also came along. Remember, the Jews looked down on the Samaritans, and much discord existed between the two groups. But, as you may recall, this Samaritan made sure the man was well cared for. Jesus asked, "Which of these three do you think was a neighbor to the man who fell into the hands of robbers?" (Luke 10:36). My point in highlighting this story again is that the Samaritan did not allow the animosity between his group and the Jews to keep him from helping a fellow human being in need.

We don't show love to people by being religious or merely attending church. We show love by the way we treat people—especially when they are in need. The Bible says, "Religion that God our Father accepts as pure and faultless is this: to look after orphans and widows in their distress and to keep oneself from being polluted by the world" (James 1:27).

Our Worth Is Not Measured by What We Own

People who are wealthy may feel they are too important to be around people who are poor, but this kind of attitude simply shows that the wealthy can be poor in what really matters. Similarly, extremely intelligent people may feel they are too good to spend time with those who barely finished high school. Likewise, a person who is gifted in many ways may look down on someone who doesn't seem to have much talent at all. These attitudes show that these people desperately lack understanding in matters that are important to God. To Him, our worth is not measured by money or possessions, intellect or education, gifts or talents, or other external abilities or trappings. God sees our heart. Loving Him and loving people is what is most important to Him.

God doesn't measure the same way people do. We are all equal to Him. He doesn't see one person as more important than another. He meets each of us where we are and loves us into wholeness. Let's all try to treat everyone as special, because God created us all, and each of us is special to Him. One of the best ways we can serve God is by being good to His people.

PART 4

God's Love Triumphs over All

CHAPTER 16

"It's Just Too Hard!"

Our greatest weakness lies in giving up. The most certain way to succeed is always to try just one more time.

Thomas Edison

One statement I hear probably more than any other when it comes to loving people who are hard to love or forgiving someone who has hurt them is "It's just too hard!" This cannot be true, because God will never command us to do something that is too hard to do. Some things may be hard, but they are not *too* hard. I believe God anoints (empowers) His people to do difficult things at times. He comes alongside us and helps us do anything He asks us to do. If we believe it is too hard, we have quit before we have even tried. But if we believe that, with God's help, we can do anything we need to do, then we are well on our way to success. All that remains is simply to act on what we need to do. God's Word tells us that nothing God commands us to do is too hard: "For this commandment which I command you this day is not too difficult for you, nor is it far off" (Deuteronomy 30:11 AMPC).

The apostle Paul writes, "I can do all things through Christ who strengthens me" (Philippians 4:13 NKJV). In the Amplified Bible, Classic Edition, this reads: "I have strength for all things in Christ Who empowers me [I am ready for anything and equal to anything through Him Who infuses inner strength into me; I am

> Thinking something too hard is what makes it too hard.

self-sufficient in Christ's sufficiency]." If we train ourselves to think we can do all things through Christ, we will find that nothing God asks us to do is too hard. Thinking something is too hard is what makes it too hard.

There are some things that are not only too hard—the Bible tells us they are impossible. Jesus says, "The things that are impossible with people are possible with God" (Luke 18:27 NASB).

The Deception of Excuses

When God commands us to do something and we say, "It's too hard," we are making an excuse, and excuses are deceptive. I once heard that an excuse is "a reason stuffed with a lie," and I agree.

In chapter 10, we talked about not being critical of other people or judging them and gossiping about them. We also talked about not giving opinions based on nothing other than what we think. And we find in Romans 2:1 this exhortation: "You, therefore, have no excuse, you who pass judgment on someone else, for at whatever point you judge another, you are condemning yourself, because you who pass judgment do the same things."

When we first read Romans 2:1, we may think, *No way, I don't do what they are doing!* But if we are truthful and stop making excuses for our behavior, we find that God's Word is right, as it always is. We look at others through a magnifying glass, which emphasizes their faults, but we make excuses for ourselves and view our behavior through rose-colored glasses, which make everything look pretty.

Jesus asks, "How can you say to your brother, 'Let me take the speck out of your eye,' when all the time there is a plank in your own eye?" (Matthew 7:4). It is amazing how often we focus on other people's faults and fail to see our own. Most of the time, I believe this is because we easily find an excuse for our shortcomings, but of course we see no excuse for what other people do.

Our excuses deceive us, and when we are deceived, we are believing lies. The devil wants us to stay busy focusing on other people's faults instead of loving them, while at the same time being blind to our own faults, lest we repent and allow God to change us.

What Is Your Excuse?

> Enter through the narrow gate; for wide is the gate and spacious and broad is the way that leads away to destruction, and many are those who are entering through it. But the gate is narrow (contracted by pressure) and the way is straitened and compressed that leads away to life, and few are those who find it.
>
> Matthew 7:13–14 AMPC

As you can see from these verses, Jesus has set before us two paths to travel through life, and we must choose one. He offers us a narrow path, which, although it is "contracted by pressure," leads to life. He also offers us a broad path that is easier to travel but leads to destruction. Our temptation is to take the easy way, but it is not the best way. This could be a place where many people would use the excuse "It is just too hard."

It is interesting that the narrow path, the one that leads to life, includes pressure. This is because the devil will do anything he can do to prevent us from taking the path that leads to a life we can enjoy. Notice that there are few who take the narrow path, but many take the broad path, not realizing, I'm sure, that it will lead to destruction, even though they have been warned.

> We should not simply live for the moment, because it passes in the blink of an eye.

If we choose to do the hard thing now, we will reap an abundant harvest (the fruit or results of our choices) in eternity. But if we take the easy path now, we will experience destruction and misery in eternity. We should begin now to live for eternity. We should not simply live for the moment, because it passes in the blink of an eye, and we are left with the consequences and results of the choices we made in it.

Start listening to yourself and ask God to show you when you make an excuse for not doing what is right. People say, "I know I shouldn't do this, but…" "I know I shouldn't eat this, but…" "I know I shouldn't buy this now, but…" We often know what God would have us do, but we make excuses and do something else anyway. Why then are we surprised when our harvest is not good?

Jesus tells a parable in Luke 14:16–20 about how we allow excuses to keep us from experiencing the good that God has prepared for us:

> A certain man was preparing a great banquet and invited many guests. At the time of the banquet he sent his servant to tell those who had been invited, "Come, for everything now is ready."
>
> But they all alike began to make excuses. The first said, "I have just bought a field, and I must go and see it. Please excuse me."
>
> Another said, "I have just bought five yoke of oxen, and I'm on my way to try them out. Please excuse me."
>
> Still another said, "I just got married, so I can't come."

Everyone in this story had an excuse, none of which was valid enough to miss the great banquet that had been prepared for them.

Jesus is preparing a great banquet in heaven for those who travel the narrow path, and He also has earthly blessings in store for those who walk obediently with Him. So be sure you don't make useless excuses and miss the blessings God has in store for you while you are on earth and when you get to heaven. The Gospel of Matthew repeatedly speaks of banquets and feasts being present in the heavenly kingdom (Matthew 8:11; 22:1–14; 25:1–13). I don't want to miss them, do you?

Now is the time to make the right decisions and believe that nothing God tells us to do is too hard, because all things are possible with Him (Matthew 19:26).

Easy Ways to Love People

Loving People with Your Thoughts

How do you think about someone who is not your favorite person, someone who grates on you or is hard for you to love? Our thoughts begin a process that our words and actions carry out. I encourage you to discipline yourself to intentionally think good thoughts about people you find challenging. Find at least three qualities

> Our thoughts begin a process that our words and actions carry out.

about them that are positive, and think about those qualities. Pray about what irritates you, and remember that you probably irritate someone yourself.

Just this week, someone hurt me by accusing me of things that were not accurate. She didn't know the whole story and made assumptions that were not true. I didn't try to defend myself, because I trust God to do that, but I am praying for her each day and remembering that she has problems rooted in her abusive childhood that she has not yet been willing to deal with.

I wish we would become more merciful in our thoughts toward others. More mercy would make the world a much better place. There are many reasons to show mercy. Here are just a few:

- Be merciful because God instructs you to do so (Luke 6:36).
- Be merciful because God is merciful to you (Hebrews 4:15–16).
- Be merciful to increase your own peace (Jude 2).
- Be merciful because you will need mercy in the future (Matthew 5:7).

When we are harsh in our opinions of and attitudes toward other people, our heart becomes hard. This adversely affects our ability to hear from God and enjoy His presence. The Holy Spirit is gentle like a dove and is offended by anger, arguing, harshness, and a critical spirit.

> Being generous in every way enlarges your heart.

Being generous in every way, including mercy, enlarges your heart. When you live this way, your capacity to love becomes larger and this pleases God.

An unloving, unkind thought about someone may come to your mind, but that doesn't mean you have to keep it and meditate on it. Remember, the Holy Spirit gives you the power to "destroy arguments and every lofty opinion raised against the knowledge of God, and take every thought captive to obey Christ" (2 Corinthians 10:5 ESV). If you will begin to think kind and loving thoughts about people, you will begin to feel kind and loving toward them. Paul teaches us to "Set your minds on things above, not on earthly things" (Colossians 3:2). The amplification of this verse in the Amplified Bible, Classic Edition says that we are not only to set our minds on things above, but to "keep them set." Paul also writes in Philippians 4:8 a powerful instruction about how we are to think: "Finally, brothers and sisters, whatever is true, whatever is noble, whatever is right, whatever is pure, whatever is lovely, whatever is admirable—if anything is excellent or praiseworthy—think about such things."

Loving People with Your Words

We can choose to say something nice about people even if we would prefer to say something unkind. Disciplining our words shows spiritual maturity, but speaking without thinking about the weight or possible impact of our words is immature. We can overcome evil with good not only in our actions but also with the words we speak (Romans 12:21). There are plenty of people saying unkind and unloving words about others, and we, as God's representatives, don't need to join them. We need to overcome evil by saying something good. Words have power, and we need to fill the atmosphere with positive power everywhere we go.

> Choose to say something nice about people.

The words we speak have a lot to do with determining our level of joy. Negative, sour, critical, slanderous words leave a heaviness in our spirit and hinder joy. But positive, beautiful, loving words fill us with joy. People often say, "I wish I had more joy" or "I wish I had more peace," but no one gets joy by wishing. However, we do have the ability to create both joy and peace in our lives by having and using the mind of Christ (1 Corinthians 2:16) and by using our words to speak positive, uplifting words about people, ourselves, and our future.

Loving People with Your Prayers

I deeply appreciate the people who pray for me. Prayer is one of the most powerful forces on earth. Through it, we have the privilege of being invited into God's presence anytime and asking for anything that is according to His will. The Bible says to bless and pray for our enemies (Luke 6:27–28). Therefore, one way we can love people who are hard for us to love is by praying for them.

Just imagine how angry it makes the devil when he works hard to get us to hate someone, but instead of doing that, we pray for them and pray for ourselves, asking God to enable us to show them love. The devil is our enemy, and we are soldiers in God's army, so we must learn how to fight with love so we can win the spiritual battles we face.

Make a list of all the people who irritate you, who have hurt your feelings or offended you, and who are difficult for you to love. Make a commitment to pray for them daily. It is difficult to pray for someone and continue to have ill feelings toward them. Let God change your heart first, and then perhaps He will change the one you find hard to love.

> Pray daily for all the people who are difficult for you to love.

Loving People with Your Material Goods

I don't know of anyone who doesn't enjoy receiving a gift. One way to fight the devil when he tries to get you not to love someone is to do things for that person. Buy them a present, give them a gift card, or help them in some practical way. It may not be something you feel like doing, but you can do it on purpose, and your loving action will break the power of the enemy. On more than one occasion, God has led me to give a favorite possession to someone who had hurt me or someone I learned had spoken unkindly about me, and I can testify that doing so broke the power of bitterness and offense and brought freedom to me. Generosity is full of power and defeats the devil. Generous people are blessed.

Here are just some of the promises God's Word makes to those who are generous:

- Generous people will be blessed (Proverbs 22:9).
- God delivers them in their time of trouble (Psalm 41:1).
- He protects them and keeps them alive (Psalm 41:2).
- Whatever they give will be given back to them many times over (Luke 6:38).
- When they are generous, they are lending to the Lord, and He will reward them (Proverbs 19:17).
- Jesus said that it is more blessed to give than to receive (Acts 20:35).

My personal belief is that being generous is one of the wisest and best things we can do for others and for ourselves. I believe generous people are happy people, and they put a smile on God's face. If you still have questions about giving to those who are hard to love, remember that God says the sun shines on the just and the unjust (Matthew 5:45), and the goodness of God leads people to repentance (Romans 2:4). You might just find your enemies repenting if you will be good to them when you think they don't deserve it.

Maybe It's Not So Hard After All

I hope that as you have read this chapter, you have realized that loving people is not as difficult as it may seem. Even when people are hard to love, you can love them in ways that are easy. A loving thought is easy. A prayer is easy. Giving your material goods may require a little more effort, but God always gives us the grace to do what He asks us to do if we are willing to do it.

It is important to believe that with God's help you can love people who are hard to love. Success in any area begins with right thinking. As long as we think, *I can't do that; it is just too hard*, we won't be able to do it. Stop thinking it is hard and begin to think, *I can do whatever God asks me to do.*

CHAPTER 17

For the Love of God

A test of your love for God is to examine your love for others.

Henry Blackaby, *Experiencing God Day by Day*

Do you love God?

The proof of our love for Him requires more than words. Jesus says that if we love Him, we will obey Him (John 14:15). He didn't say that if we obey Him, He will love us; He said that He loved us and died for us while we were still sinners (Romans 5:8). But our love for Him will produce obedience.

This chapter's opening quote says that one of the tests of our love for God is our love for others. This is a sobering thought. We may love those who love us, which requires little effort or discipline, but to love those who are hard to love and may not love us back is something else entirely. This Scripture passage says it all:

> One of the tests of our love for God is our love for others.

If you love those who love you, what credit is that to you? Even sinners love those who love them. And if you do good to those who are good to you, what credit is that to you? Even sinners do that. And if you lend to those from whom you expect repayment, what credit is that to you?

Even sinners lend to sinners, expecting to be repaid in full. But love your enemies, do good to them, and lend to them without expecting to get anything back. Then your reward will be great, and you will be children of the Most High, because he is kind to the ungrateful and wicked. Be merciful, just as your Father is merciful.

Luke 6:32–36

Anytime we do something for someone and expect to be paid back, what we are giving them is not a gift, but more like a bribe (a gift, money, or a favor given in order to get something from another person). If you do good to a person and they do good back to you, it's fine unless you did it for the purpose of wanting them to repay you.

Many people think they are being kind and generous at times, but they become angry when the person to whom they extended kindness fails to repay the supposed favor. In that case, the favor really wasn't a favor at all, because a true favor cannot be earned or deserved.

Scriptures such as Luke 6:32–36 are important because they help us to think about why we do what we do. What is our motive for the good we do? Do you become offended when you do something for someone and they don't do anything for you? What if you invite them to your party, but later they have a party and don't invite you? What if you buy them an expensive birthday or Christmas gift, and they buy you something very inexpensive that you think they put no effort into choosing for you? How does that affect you? Or, what if they don't buy you a gift at all? Are you willing to keep treating them well simply because it is right—and trust God to take care of you?

If you were to receive an inheritance from a relative and tithe a large sum of that money to your church, would you expect special treatment from the pastor as a result? Or would you be able to give it to the Lord, expecting nothing in return?

> God expects us to do more than people who do not know Him.

God expects us to do more than people who do not know Him would do, because His Holy Spirit lives in us and enables us to go beyond what seems normal, easy, or expected. We can act in a more excellent way or go the extra mile. We can love those who are hard to love. We can love people even if they don't love us back. Luke 6:35 tells us that God is kind to the ungrateful and the wicked, and we can be kind too.

We often pray to be like Jesus. Do we really want to be like He is, or do we simply say this in order to sound spiritual? Have you ever really thought about how it would change your life if you were like Jesus? I must admit that I haven't, but I am encouraged to do so after reading Luke 6:32–36. This doesn't sound like a very exciting way to live, but tucked in the middle of these verses is a promise we don't want to miss. It says in verse 35 that if we do live this way, our "reward will be great." We love rewards, but I am inclined to think we probably will miss a lot of rewards God would like to give us because we don't obey Him when doing so is difficult.

The apostle Peter writes something that is even more difficult to want to do than what we read about in Luke 6:

> For one is regarded favorably (is approved, acceptable, and thankworthy) if, as in the sight of God, he endures the pain of unjust suffering. [After all] what kind of glory [is there in it] if, when you do wrong and are punished for it, you take it patiently? But if you bear patiently with suffering [which results] when you do right and that is undeserved,

it is acceptable and pleasing to God. For even to this were
you called [it is inseparable from your vocation]. For Christ
also suffered for you, leaving you [His personal] example,
so that you should follow in His footsteps.

1 Peter 2:19–21 AMPC

Let me state from the beginning of our focus on these verses
that it is not our undeserved suffering that is pleasing to God. It
is bearing with the suffering patiently that pleases Him, because
this makes us like Jesus.

I remember the first time I heard these scriptures as I was listening to a recorded sermon. When I heard that I had been called
to live a life of enduring unjust suffering with a good attitude, I
must admit I wasn't too thrilled. First Peter 1:19–21 is another
passage of Scripture that makes clear that to live as Jesus lived,
to be like Him, requires loving those who are hard to love, loving our enemies and those who treat us unjustly—and doing it
with a good attitude. Look again at verse 21: "For Christ also suffered for you, leaving you [His personal] example, so that you
should follow in His footsteps." Wow. Are we ready to do that?
We should think long and hard before saying yes.

I want to mention again that God does not require us to allow
people to abuse us, but He does require us to forgive those who
hurt us. You may need to stay away from someone who has
become dangerous to you, but you can still forgive and pray for
that person. You don't have to like someone in order to love them.

I have recently forgiven two people who hurt and disappointed
me. I don't like the way they are behaving. I don't like the fact that
they are not taking responsibility for their behavior. And I don't
like them right now, but I do love them with the love of Christ,
and I am praying for them daily. I would help them if they needed

help I could give them, and I will bless them by not spreading to others what they have done. We can and should forgive and love others in obedience to Jesus (Matthew 18:21–22; John 13:34).

> You don't have to like someone in order to love them.

The disciples had three years with Jesus to learn His ways and see firsthand how He handled situations. After Jesus rose from the dead and before He ascended to heaven, He told them that their job was to go out into the world, emulate what they had learned from Him, and teach it to others (Matthew 28:6–7, 16–20). We are still learning today from the writings they left us, but the question before us is, How far are we willing to go? What are we willing to do for the love of God?

When someone knows you are a Christian, your behavior comes under scrutiny. People want to see if you are authentic and if you really live in your daily life what you say you believe. One person can affect many people in a positive way or in a negative way.

> When someone knows you are a Christian, your behavior comes under scrutiny.

> For just as through the disobedience of the one man the many were made sinners, so also through the obedience of the one man the many will be made righteous.
>
> Romans 5:19

We have a greater influence on one another than we may think. Sin was introduced into the world through one man, Adam, and righteousness came through one man, Jesus. Don't discount yourself, thinking that your behavior doesn't matter much, because it does affect people, and we should keep in mind that we are ambassadors for Jesus Christ. We are His personal representatives (2 Corinthians 5:20).

More Love = More Obedience

I believe the more we love God, the more obedient to Him we will be. I know that as I have grown in my knowledge of God and in my love for Him, I have also grown in my obedience to His commands.

What does it mean to obey God? Mary Fairchild writes on LearnReligions.org that "According to *Holman's Illustrated Bible Dictionary*, a succinct definition of biblical obedience is 'to hear God's Word and act accordingly'" and concludes that "biblical obedience to God means to hear, trust, submit and surrender to God and his Word."

Today we have an abundance of knowledge available to us, but knowing something doesn't necessarily mean we are doing what we know to do. God's Word says that to know what is right to do and not do it is sin (James 4:17). If we know we should forgive someone who has hurt us and refuse to do so, it is sin. If we know we should not gossip, but we continue doing so, it is sin.

> Knowing we should forgive someone and refusing to do so is sinful.

The apostle Paul said that he received mercy for his many sins because he acted in ignorance before he found Christ (1 Timothy 1:13). I often tell people who attend one of my seminars that when they leave, they will be responsible for more than they were responsible for when they came simply because they will be accountable for what they learn. I think it is unwise to ever walk into a church service or teaching seminar unless you have already made up your mind that you will not only hear but you will also *do*, with God's help, what you are taught to do, assuming, of course, that the information you receive is correct.

I have grown in my knowledge of God's Word over the years, and I have grown in my obedience to God simultaneously. As I have grown in my love for Jesus, I have grown in my obedience to His commands. I frequently come up against things that are hard to do, but I have found that I will do them for no other reason except that I love Jesus.

In John 21:15–19, Jesus asked Peter three times if he loved Him, and each time Peter said that he did love Him. Jesus responded with "Feed my sheep" (v. 17). Peter was grieved that the Lord asked him the same question three times, but perhaps He did so because it's easy to say yes to something without counting the cost of actually doing it. Jesus wanted Peter to know that loving Him meant serving others and working for their benefit.

When Jesus asked Peter if he loved Him, He used the word *agape*, which is the kind of unconditional love God has for us. But Peter answered with another word for love, *phileo*, the Greek word that refers to a brotherly type of love or the love between friends. In response to Jesus' question, Peter said, "You know that I *phileo* You." Perhaps Jesus was trying to move Peter from *phileo* to *agape*. When an instruction or question is repeated, it is because it is important for us to understand what is really being said. Jesus wanted Peter to understand that loving Him would mean sacrifice. I often wonder if we understand this today.

Jesus further tells Peter that when he was young, he did as he pleased, but when he grew old another would carry him where he did not wish to go (John 21:18). I believe this means that when Peter was a young believer, he walked in his own will, but that as he matured in Christ and grew in his love for Him, he would be required to do things he would not naturally want to do.

The Blessings of Obedience

Any time we do something that is hard to do, it helps us if we also know the reward that will come as a result. Knowing that staying strong, having muscle instead of fat, and continuing to wear the same size clothing is the reward for working out helps me on days when I don't really want to exercise.

Looking forward to payday helps us go to work day after day. Likewise, knowing that obedience brings rewards helps us continue being obedient when it gets hard. We should not do it for reward, but because of our love for Jesus. However, God's Word does tell us that there will be rewards for obedience. Here are a few scriptures that give us that promise:

> If you fully obey the Lord your God and carefully follow all his commands I give you today, the Lord your God will set you high above all the nations on earth.
>
> Deuteronomy 28:1

> Walk in obedience to all that the Lord your God has commanded you, so that you may live and prosper and prolong your days in the land that you will possess.
>
> Deuteronomy 5:33

> Keep this Book of the Law always on your lips; meditate on it day and night, so that you may be careful to do everything written in it. Then you will be prosperous and successful.
>
> Joshua 1:8

Blessed are all who fear the Lord, who walk in obedience to him.

Psalm 128:1

Whatever you do, work at it with all your heart, as working for the Lord, not for human masters, since you know that you will receive an inheritance from the Lord as a reward. It is the Lord Christ you are serving.

Colossians 3:23–24

God also tells us in several places in His Word that if we obey Him in giving, it will come back to us many times over (Proverbs 22:9; Luke 6:38; Acts 20:35). Once again, I don't recommend giving to get, but it is still good to know that giving does produce a reward.

God wants us to look forward to the rewards He has stored up for us. Some of them we receive here on earth, and others are reserved for us when we get to heaven.

> Obedience proves our love for God.

Jesus says He is coming soon and His rewards are with Him (Revelation 22:12). He also says He will "reward each person according to what they have done" (Matthew 16:27). Obedience pays wonderful rewards and proves our love for God.

CHAPTER 18

What in the World Is Going On?

For the grace of God has appeared that offers salvation to all people. It teaches us to say "No" to ungodliness and worldly passions, and to live self-controlled, upright and godly lives in this present age.

Titus 2:11–12

I closed the previous chapter with a section on the blessings of obedience to God's Word. When we obey His Word, we are blessed, and when we do not obey His Word, we are not blessed. This is true for us as individuals, and it is true in marriages, families, nations, and the world at large today. Regard for God's Word seems to be at an all-time low. Some people are simply ignorant of what it teaches, some mock and make fun of it, and some are downright hostile toward it. As we think about what is going on in the world today, I believe we are currently seeing the consequences of this lack of respect of God's Word in many ways.

Think about it: Moral values are rapidly declining, fewer people are going to church, and integrity is something few people even understand. Honor and faithfulness are fading character traits. Many people are greedy, selfish, rebellious, and haters of what is good (Romans 1:28–31).

Random acts of violence are taking place with increased frequency, crime is rising dramatically, perversion abounds, young people are killing other young people and themselves, and bad things people could not have imagined just twenty or thirty years ago are happening regularly.

We have to ask: What exactly is going on? Why does the world seem to be spinning out of control in a negative direction? We are in the midst of a raging spiritual battle between good and evil, and many people are choosing evil. Are we living in what the Bible calls the last days or the end times? If we look at the signs the Bible tells us to watch for (Mark 13:4–13), they certainly seem to be prevalent today, but Jesus is clear that regarding His return, "no one knows, not even the angels of heaven, but My Father only" (Matthew 24:36 NKJV).

Paul describes the last days in his second letter to Timothy:

> But mark this: There will be terrible times in the last days. People will be lovers of themselves, lovers of money, boastful, proud, abusive, disobedient to their parents, ungrateful, unholy, without love, unforgiving, slanderous, without self-control, brutal, not lovers of the good, treacherous, rash, conceited, lovers of pleasure rather than lovers of God—having a form of godliness but denying its power. Have nothing to do with such people.
>
> 2 Timothy 3:1–5

As I read these verses, I feel I am looking at a picture of the world today. Matthew 24:3–12 also gives us signs of the end times—wars and rumors of wars, earthquakes, famines, hatred, turning away from the faith, great deception, many people being offended, and the love of many people will grow cold because of the wickedness and lawlessness in the land. People will betray one another and hate one another. This sounds bad, but there is a piece of good news also. Matthew 24:13–14 says, "The one who stands firm to the end will be saved. And this gospel of the kingdom will be preached in the whole world as a testimony to all nations."

> I believe good things are taking place all the time.

While Satan does his worst work, we should do our best and spread the good of the gospel in every way we can. Optimistic, uplifting news is rare, but I still believe good things are taking place all the time. We simply need to be committed to spreading the positive information we know. Let me encourage you to tell people about Jesus, financially support ministries that are telling people about Jesus, and, very importantly, be an example of God's love, peace, and grace everywhere you go.

The Lines Are Blurred

Paul told Timothy to have nothing to do with people who live as he describes in 2 Timothy 3:1–5. Although he advised Timothy not to interact with such people, I am sure he spent time with unbelievers and wicked people for the purpose of speaking truth to them. We cannot hide from all the people who need to know Jesus and merely gather in our little Christian groups, criticizing and judging those who are not like we are. Spend time with unbelievers as long as you are *influencing* them and they are not *infecting* you. Today the lines between those who love God and want His will and those who are against Him are blurred. We cannot be so much like the world that people can't recognize us as belonging to God. We can and should be good to people and do random acts of kindness. We need to be gentle, forbearing, long-suffering, and patient with people, just as our Lord is with us.

Jesus' advice to us is to be in the world but not of the world (John 17:11–17; Philippians 2:15). We are not to be conformed to this world, but to be transformed by the renewal of our minds according to the Word of God (Romans 12:2). This means we should think and act according to God's Word, not according to our own selfish thoughts, feelings, or desires.

It is time for believers in Jesus Christ to take a stand, let our lights shine, and make ourselves available to God for His use. It is time to bloom where we are planted. And it is definitely time to be obedient to God's Word, no matter how we feel. I believe that God has placed each one of us where we are for the express purpose of representing Him to the world around us. God has His people everywhere, and Christians must stop hiding and being fearful of being rejected when others see that they believe in God and love Him with all their hearts.

The place God has given you to work for Him may be a neighborhood, a school, or a place of employment. Everyone has their own pulpit, even if it is a backyard fence or a desk at work. We don't all need to be behind a pulpit on a platform, but we do all need to behave as God wants us to behave.

Godly behavior will preach for us if we let it. But as I said, the lines between who is a Christian and who isn't are so blurred that recognizing the difference is becoming difficult. Frequently this is because God's people are prone to compromise because they want to fit in and not be scorned or rejected. Compromising means doing a little less than what you know to be right. That little bit is dangerous, because we often think a little bit doesn't matter, but it is often the little things that pile up and ruin our lives. Jesus didn't worry about fitting in

> Compromising means doing a little less than what you know to be right.

with the people around Him. He always seemed to stand out as different and to do right, even when it was unpopular.

As an example of how deceived people are becoming, a man I know told me about his friend, who is a Christian and is in the process of divorce. In the meantime, he is living with his girlfriend. He suggested to my friend that they fast one day a week to develop one of the fruits of the Spirit (Galatians 5:22–23). So here we have a so-called Christian man living in sin, yet thinking God will pay attention to his fasting. When asked if he didn't realize he was living in sin, he answered, "I think God understands."

What this man does not understand is that he cannot bring God down to his low level of living, because God has called us to come up higher and be like Jesus. Couples who live together before marriage have become so commonplace that doing so is frequently recommended and expected. Some parents even suggest to their children who are thinking about marriage that they live together for a while first to see if they will get along with their prospective spouse.

It is important that we remember that just because most of the people in the world act in certain ways, it doesn't make their behavior right. We should always choose to follow God's Word, not the world.

In 2018, the *Journal of Marriage and Family* published a study with a somewhat foreboding finding: Couples who lived together before marriage had a lower divorce rate in their first year of marriage, but a higher divorce rate after five years.

There are still a lot more people who don't live together before marriage than those who do, and for that I am very thankful, but the percentage of those who cohabitate outside of God's covenant of marriage is increasing yearly. If we choose to live according to

God's commands, our lives will be blessed, and if we don't, we cannot expect His blessings.

I also read that 95 percent of people engage in premarital sex, even though the Bible forbids sexual immorality, impurity, and debauchery (Galatians 5:19). Since the percentage is this high, some of you reading this book fit into that statistic, but please don't get angry and throw the book away. It is not meant to condemn you, but for all of us to see some of the reasons our world is in the condition in which it is today. God loves us and forgives us. He meets us where we are, but He doesn't want us to stay there. He wants us to grow spiritually and continually make better and better choices. I don't believe any one factor is causing the problems, but each time we stray from God's Word, it contributes to the problem and opens more doors for Satan to work evil in the world.

I recently taught a message titled "Being Godly in an Ungodly World" and spoke of the dangers of moral compromise and blending in with the world. At the end of the message, I asked people who needed to repent of such things as sexual immorality, lying, hatred, jealousy, and other unhealthy behaviors to come forward for prayer. The altar was full of people. They were three and four rows deep, and most of them were Christians. I don't say this judgmentally, but with concern and in order that we might all see the seriousness of our condition and realize how desperately change is needed. If you are going to be a Christian, then be a real one, not just one who goes to church on Sunday and then acts like the world the rest of the week.

Perhaps some people don't know any better, or they take wrong advice. Thankfully, we can be forgiven for any sin, but it is much better to avoid sin to begin with than to need forgiveness later. Sin can always be forgiven, but it does have consequences.

We may comfort ourselves by telling ourselves that God understands our sin. Even if He does, it doesn't mean He ignores it and puts His stamp of approval on it.

Another concern I have is the large number of Christians who hold unforgiveness against people who have hurt them, when the Bible clearly tells us that we must freely forgive even as Christ has forgiven us (Colossians 3:13). They remain angry instead of peaceful, have homes filled with strife even though they faithfully attend church, divorce their spouses when they have no biblical grounds to do so, and act in other ways that are not in accordance with God's Word.

The Good News

Although there are Christians who compromise with the world, there are also many committed Christians who are serious about their relationship with God and work tirelessly to love and help people. They do their best to live godly lives, they pray, they care, they have compassion toward others, and they stand firm for what is right. There are many wonderful churches that are teaching people correctly, but we need every church to be that way. We need the strong meat of God's Word for the times in which we live, but sadly, some people won't listen to it. They search for people who will preach what they *want* to hear instead of what they *need* to hear. According to 2 Timothy 4:3–4, this is another sign of the end times: "For the time will come when people will not put up with sound doctrine. Instead, to suit their own desires, they will gather around them a great number of teachers to say what their itching ears want to hear. They will turn their ears away from the truth and turn aside to myths."

The Remnant

Another piece of good news is that God always has a remnant—a small remaining quantity—of people He can count on, and I pray you are among them. Elijah thought he was the only prophet remaining who loved and obeyed God, but the Lord told him that He had seven thousand people in Israel who had not bowed their knee to Baal (1 Kings 19:18). Thank God for the remnant remaining in the earth, those who are committed to doing God's will.

I pray that you will be a person through whom God can work in the days in which we live. Ask yourself if you are more concerned with God's will than with your own will. Does your heart break with what breaks God's heart? Are you willing to sacrifice in order to be someone God can use to change the world and help get things back on His track? It is good for all of us, including me, to take a personal inventory occasionally and ask ourselves if we are still swimming upstream against the current in the world or if we are merely floating downstream with everyone else because that is easier than living according to God's ways.

In this book, I focus extensively on love and peace because I think we need love and peace in the world more than anything else. The two go together. They cannot be separated. William Gladstone is purported to have said, "We look forward to the time when the Power of Love will replace the Love of Power. Then will our world know the blessings of peace."

From Satan's Deception to God's Truth

Another story that illustrated how far from holy living we have strayed is this: A sweet and sincere girl called our office to ask a question. She said that some of her friends were doing things that were illegal, yet their lives were being amazingly blessed, and they told her they felt that God's grace was covering them. Her question for us was whether or not that was true. Of course, we told her it wasn't, but it does depict how Satan operates. He can tempt us to do wrong and then arrange for us to be blessed to make it seem that what we are doing is okay. But in the end, a reckoning will come.

> It is better to be in God's will and have nothing than to be out of His will with many material blessings.

It is better to be in God's will and have nothing than to be out of His will with many material blessings.

God's Word teaches us, "Do not fret because of those who are evil or be envious of those who do wrong; for like the grass they will soon wither, like green plants they will soon die away" (Psalm 37:1–2). Even in the midst of the negative circumstances in our world, there are also good things, and I believe God wants us to be joyful and enjoy our lives. We need to be aware of the problems, but we don't have to focus on them all the time. My primary goal in this book is to encourage every person to do their part. If enough of us do our part, we can win the war, because good always overcomes evil.

Luke 4:1–13 recounts the time when the Holy Spirit led Jesus into the wilderness to be tempted by the devil. During one of those temptations, Satan told Jesus that if He would simply worship him, he would give Him all the kingdoms of the world, along with all their authority and splendor. The devil clearly said, "It has been given to me, and I can give it to anyone I want to. If you worship me, it will all be yours" (Luke 4:6–7). Of course, Jesus resisted the temptation, but not everyone does. Many people compromise in order to have the things of the world. They seem to prosper, but such prosperity is not from God. True prosperity includes peace, joy, and righteousness, along with having our needs met and being able to generously help others who are in need. People can have possessions and financial resources yet have no peace or joy. They are selfish and love no one other than themselves, and they certainly are not living righteous lives. We should not assume that just because someone seems prosperous that God has blessed them. Many people are deceived by riches (Mark 4:19).

When Adam committed sin through disobeying God, he turned his God-given authority over to Satan. This is why the devil can say that everything in the world is his to give to whomever he chooses. But Jesus defeated Satan and took back the authority God originally delegated to us. The authority and power God has given us over the devil is available through Christ to all who believe and follow God's will. Yes, we have authority and power over the devil, but it must be exercised, and only those who are living according to God's will to the best of their ability can do so.

When we are deceived, we believe lies. Those lies then become our truth, and we act according to what we believe. Deception will increase in the last days, and the Bible tells us that if God doesn't shorten the days, even the very elect will be deceived (Matthew 24:22–24). We need to know God's Word and have great discernment. We also need to exercise wisdom in all we do, and we need to pray to avoid being trapped by deception.

When I began to seriously study God's Word, I began learning that I had believed many of Satan's lies, which prevented me from enjoying the good life that Jesus died for me to live. One of the biggest lies I remember holding on to for years was that because I had been sexually abused by my father, I was damaged goods, and that I would always have a second-rate life. I had yet to learn the truth of 2 Corinthians 5:17, which states, "If anyone is in Christ, the new creation has come; the old has gone, the new is here!" Jesus is a Restorer of all things. There is nothing broken that He cannot fix.

The Bible contains multiple instructions for us to let go of what lies behind us, but these are two of the most outstanding:

> Forget the former things; do not dwell on the past. See, I am doing a new thing! Now it springs up; do you not perceive it? I am making a way in the wilderness and streams in the wasteland.
>
> Isaiah 43:18–19

> Brothers and sisters, I do not consider myself yet to have taken hold of it. But one thing I do: Forgetting what is behind and straining toward what is ahead, I press on toward the goal to win the prize for which God has called me heavenward in Christ Jesus.
>
> Philippians 3:13–14

How refreshing and exciting it is to realize the truth that when we are born again (accept Jesus as our Savior and Lord), we get a brand-new beginning. We get a new life.

Many of the lies that Satan tries to get us to believe are lies about God's love for us, His forgiveness, our future, our worth and value, our purpose, and our abilities. He wants us to be guilt-ridden, anxious, joyless, and hopeless, but we can defeat him as we learn God's Word, believe it, and act on it.

God's Word is the only consistent source of truth. We cannot get our education from television, social media, the news media, or Hollywood, because these sources are often used to spread the very deceptions we are talking about. I urge you to commit to taking time

> God's Word is the only consistent source of truth.

to know God's Word and to believe it more than you believe any other source of information.

CHAPTER 19

Love Wins

The night is nearly over; the day is almost here. So let us put aside the deeds of darkness and put on the armor of light.

Romans 13:12

You and I are living in dark times. Sin abounds, and I think we can say that the world is growing darker all the time. Darkness is a reference to evil, and light is a reference to righteousness. The prince of darkness is the devil, but Jesus is the light of the world (John 8:12). Darkness cannot put out light, but light can swallow up darkness. Just think of walking into a dark room and flipping on a light switch. Immediately all the dark is swallowed up and the room is filled with light.

Those of us who belong to the light—to Jesus—can let our lights shine more brightly and conquer the darkness. Jesus says whoever follows (obeys) Him "will never walk in darkness" (John 8:12). He also says that we are the light of the world and we should let our lights shine, meaning to represent Him well in the world. We are taught to follow in Jesus' footsteps (1 Peter 2:21) and to be conformed to His image (Romans 8:29), and it is important for the world to see Christlike fruit displayed in our lives.

> You are the light of the world. A town built on a hill cannot be hidden. Neither do people light a lamp and

> put it under a bowl. Instead they put it on its stand, and
> it gives light to everyone in the house. In the same way,
> let your light shine before others, that they may see your
> good deeds and glorify your Father in heaven.
>
> Matthew 5:14–16

Is your light shining? Does it need to be turned up brighter? We should not hide our light, but let it shine before others, so they can see our good deeds (love) and glorify God. True love always manifests in good deeds. If love consists of only words with no action, it isn't the kind of love God wants us to have. God loves us, and He is constantly doing things for us.

I believe "the armor of light" mentioned in Romans 13:12 refers to love and every kind of godly behavior. Good always overcomes evil (Romans 12:21). When someone does evil against us and we treat them the same way they treated us, we give the devil exactly what he is hoping for: hate and more hate. But if we repay evil with good, we conquer our enemy, Satan.

> If we repay evil with good, we conquer Satan.

I also believe love is the highest and most effective type of spiritual warfare we can wage. Ephesians 6:10–18 teaches us to put on our spiritual armor—righteousness, truth, peace, faith, salvation, "the sword of the Spirit, which is the word of God" (v. 17)—and to cover everything with prayer in order to defeat the principalities and powers arrayed against us. And I believe the armor of light (love) is another piece of the spiritual armor. Love is more effective than any of them, although each piece is necessary.

The reason God tells us to love our enemies, pray for them, and bless them is that when we do, we defeat Satan. The devil is filled with hatred and lies, and he cannot love. He is afraid of our ability to love others and will do anything he can do to stop love from flowing. He desires disunity, strife, bitterness, hatred, arguing, anger, and resentment in our lives and relationships, but love is the antidote to all of these. Love is incredibly powerful, and Satan is afraid of it.

Negative Emotions Can Hinder Love

When someone treats us unjustly or hurts us, our emotions will try to lead us to take revenge and do to them what they have done to us. We may want to punish them in some way so they will know they cannot get away with treating us harmfully. But this is not the way God wants us to behave. This is where we must choose whether to follow emotions or to obey God's Word.

When we do right while it feels wrong, we make spiritual progress, meaning that we are growing spiritually. As children grow, they often have what we call growing pains. Their legs may ache, or they may experience other sensations as they mature. As Christians, we go through a similar process, except that it happens in our soul instead of our body.

I remember when Dave taught me how to play golf. The way you must grip and swing the club feels completely wrong, but the club must be held that way in order for the ball to go in the right direction. If you hold the club in a way that feels comfortable, the ball goes all wrong. Our walk with God is often like that. In order to get the right result, the one that God wants, we may need to do things that feel wrong to us. They may not be comfortable, but they will produce the desired result.

For example, it might not be comfortable to say to someone, "I'm sorry we argued. I was wrong, and you were right." Admitting you were wrong will produce the result God desires. It will help you maintain unity, preserve your love walk, and show humility, all of which are important.

> Admitting you were wrong will produce the result that God desires.

James 1:22 says that if we hear God's Word and don't do it, it is because we deceive ourselves through reasoning that is contrary to the truth. We know what we should do, but we find a reason to think that not doing it is all right, thereby excusing our disobedience. There should never be an excuse to disobey God.

When I become angry over something Dave has said or done, I don't want to talk to him or even be in the same room with him, but I refuse to let my emotions control me, because I know they will lead me toward destruction. Although sometimes I need a cooling-off period, I make the decision to talk to Dave even if I don't want to, and I refuse to avoid him, because I know division is what the devil wants.

What about your emotions? Do you let them prevent you from doing what you know you should do? If you tend to follow your emotions, you can change that today by making the decision to do so. You can feel your feelings, but you cannot follow them and be a mature Christian. Always make the decision to do what God wants you to do, and you will be victorious in life. Emotions are deceptive. Sometimes they are good, and other times they are bad. We all have them, and they will not go away. We simply need to learn how to manage them and not let them manage us.

Evil people who are filled with darkness are not comfortable around Christians filled with light for fear that their sins will be exposed. Your very presence as a believer makes those living in darkness uncomfortable. So, don't be surprised if you find that nonbelieving people who once accepted you now reject you. They are not really rejecting you; they are rejecting Jesus in you.

God has rescued us from the kingdom of darkness and transferred us into the kingdom of light (Colossians 1:12–15). When a person is born again (accepts Jesus as their Savior and Lord), they immediately begin to see the light. Prior to being saved, a person may do many evil things and not realize they are evil or be convicted by doing them. But after the new birth, that same behavior will make them uncomfortable as they receive the conviction and guidance of the Holy Spirit and begin to discern right from wrong.

It will be hard for that person to intentionally do what is wrong without feeling convicted. Before I got serious in my relationship with God, I watched whatever I wanted to watch on television and went to all kinds of movies. But after making a deeper commitment to God, I started noticing that some of the shows and movies I had watched previously made me uncomfortable. I just didn't feel right about watching them. No one told me to stop watching them; the Holy Spirit was letting me know in my heart that they weren't good for me or pleasing to God.

There are things we do without thinking, and then we realize we have made a mistake. We can admit and confess what we have done, repent, and receive forgiveness. But when someone repeatedly does what they fully understand is wrong and against God's will, the question must be asked: Does that person truly know God?

> Whoever says, "I know him," but does not do what he commands is a liar, and the truth is not in that person.
>
> 1 John 2:4

> No one born (begotten) of God [deliberately, knowingly, and habitually] practices sin, for God's nature abides

in him [His principle of life, the divine sperm, remains permanently within him]; and he cannot practice sinning because he is born (begotten) of God.

1 John 3:9 AMPC

First John 3:9 has been very helpful to me in understanding the difference between accidental sin and purposeful sin. If I'm waiting for a parking space and someone else rushes in front of me and takes the space that I was clearly waiting on, I may immediately feel angry and want to yell at them. The Holy Spirit will make me aware that my behavior is not right, and I can decide to repent and change my behavior. This is quite different from what 1 John 3:9 is talking about. People who "deliberately, knowingly, and habitually" practice sin cannot have God's nature abiding in them.

> People who sin deliberately cannot have God's nature abiding in them.

Compromise

Compromising means doing a little less than what you know to be right. Today, the world is filled with compromise, and sometimes the church is too. One thing compromise does, which we don't always realize, is open a door for the enemy to work in our lives. Paul writes that we should "have nothing to do with the fruitless deeds of darkness, but rather expose them" (Ephesians 5:11). We should be able to see a distinct difference between unbelievers and those who believe in Jesus Christ.

Paul also says, "Do not be yoked together with unbelievers. For what do righteousness and wickedness have in common? Or what fellowship can light have with darkness?" (2 Corinthians 6:14). In practical terms, this means, among other instructions, don't go into business with an unbeliever and don't marry an unbeliever. Even dating an unbeliever is unwise. I am fully aware, even as I write this, that many people reading this book won't like these statements. I don't make them to anger anyone, but because they are true. If you are involved in any kind of compromise, my desire is to keep you out of trouble. It is a minister's job to tell people what they need to hear, not what they want to hear. You may date an unbeliever thinking you will change them. That does sometimes happen, but if they don't change before you marry, chances are they won't change after you marry. So, in my opinion, it is best not to get involved unless they show signs of being willing to change early in the relationship.

I have a granddaughter who began dating an unbeliever, but early in the relationship she asked him to go to church with her. He did and he loved it. He made a commitment to Christ and is now a strong believer. I doubt she would have dated him very long had he refused to be open to a relationship with Christ. She put Jesus first in her life, as we all should.

The only reason we should spend time with unbelievers is for the purpose of showing them the love of God and hopefully eventually being able to share the truth with them. Jesus ate with sinners, but He never compromised the truth when He was with them. He loved them, and His love often changed them. Hopefully, we can have the same effect on those who walk in darkness.

Are You Ready for War?

The Bible tells us that we are in a war (2 Corinthians 10:3–5; Ephesians 6:10–18). We are soldiers in God's army, and our unseen enemy is Satan (and his demon hosts), but God is on our side. God has given us power and authority over Satan; however, we must exercise the authority He gives us in order for it to be effective: "Behold! I have given you authority and power to trample upon serpents and scorpions, and [physical and mental strength and ability] over all the power that the enemy [possesses]; and nothing shall in any way harm you" (Luke 10:19 AMPC).

James 4:7 says, "Submit yourselves, then, to God. Resist the devil, and he will flee from you." Often people only quote the last half of this verse, saying, "If I resist the devil, he will flee from me." But resisting the devil does no good if we are not submitted to God in obedience to Him. We can see from this scripture how important obedience is in spiritual warfare.

God's Word probably commands us to love God and one another more than anything else. Paul writes that "The goal of our instruction is love [which springs] from a pure heart and a good conscience and a sincere faith" (1 Timothy 1:5 AMP). Wow. Everything Paul taught the people was for one purpose—to teach them to walk in faith and to love God and one another.

Unless we walk in love, we are weak and powerless against Satan. Love gives us power. Consider these true statements:

> Unless we walk in love, we are powerless against Satan.

- Without love, our prayers are weak.
- Without love, our witness is weak.
- Without love, we are unhappy.
- Without love, we are not pleasing God.
- Without love, we open a door for Satan in our lives.

In addition, without love, our faith won't work. Faith works (expresses itself) through love (Galatians 5:6). We won't put our faith in God if we don't believe He loves us. And if we don't love

Him and other people, our faith won't work. We may be doing what we think is praying in faith, but it won't produce the desired result if we don't make loving God and loving people priorities in our lives.

The War Is Spiritual

Are we really in a war? Yes, but it is a spiritual war. We cannot see it with our natural eyes, but it is real. Satan is fighting us all the time, and we need to learn to recognize his attacks and stand against them. The apostle Peter writes that we are to "withstand" the devil and to "be firm in faith [against his onset]" (1 Peter 5:9 AMPC). In other words, we are to resist him as soon as he attacks.

In the spiritual war, God provides spiritual weapons: "The weapons we fight with are not the weapons of the world. On the contrary, they have divine power to demolish strongholds" (2 Corinthians 10:4). These strongholds are mental strongholds that Satan builds in our minds through lies he tells us. When we believe lies, we are deceived, but the lies we believe become our reality, even though they are not true.

God's Word is our greatest weapon against the devil. As His Word renews our mind, we learn to think according to His truth. As we believe His Word, we are changed. We might say that the Word is our weapon and love is our protection.

By speaking God's Word, we break the strategies and plans Satan has designed against us. God even said through the prophet Jeremiah that His word is like a hammer: " 'Is not my word like fire,' declares the Lord, 'and like a hammer that breaks a rock in pieces?' " (Jeremiah 23:29).

A believer who knows God, walks in love, speaks the Word, and obeys God is dangerous to Satan. I pray you are seeing how important love is and that you will make a commitment to love not only those who are easy to love but also those who are hard to love. If you become angry, don't stay angry, and don't let your heart be filled with unforgiveness, resentment, or strife. Remain peaceful. Wear your shoes of peace, as Ephesians 6:15 instructs. We walk in our shoes, so this means to walk in peace as you go through your life. In order to do this, you will need to be humble, adaptable, and adjustable.

Another spiritual weapon God gives us is prayer. It is a powerful weapon in the spiritual realm, one we can use easily each day. I encourage you to begin today praying for your enemies and committing not to saying a bad word about them again. If the opportunity presents itself and you feel it is right for you to do, help them if they are in trouble. You will see more positive results from these loving actions than from anything else you could do.

Society may be filled with negativity, and the enemy may try to sow hatred everywhere he can, but love is the greatest force on earth, and it can change the world. Because the Holy Spirit lives in us, we have the power to love all people. Let's always remember that God loves the world so much that He "gave His only Son, so that everyone who believes in Him will not perish, but have eternal life" (John 3:16 NASB).

CONCLUSION

Hopefully by now you want and are ready to let God help you love everyone, even people who are hard to love. In your quest to learn more about love, make sure that you yourself are not the one who is hard to love. I admit that I was very hard to love for many years. Because of my abusive past, I wanted to control

> Make sure that you yourself are not the one who is hard to love.

everything and everyone, so I was only happy when I got my way. I am so grateful to God for changing me and now I can be happy even when I don't get my way.

The healing of a wounded soul begins with facing truth, so if you are hard to love, it's time to own it and ask God to heal you. Healing won't come immediately, because God changes us little by little, but we can celebrate any kind of progress and expect more to come. My book *Healing the Soul of a Woman* would be helpful if you are ready to begin a journey of inner healing.

Don't make the mistake of thinking that you cannot begin loving others more because you are hard to love. I think the more you love others, the more you will receive a harvest of healing in your own life.

I encourage you to remember that love is the greatest thing in the world and to make it a priority every day of your life. Also remember that love is not merely a feeling; it is a decision to treat people the way Jesus treats them. It involves forgiveness, praying for people, blessing them with your words, helping them if they are in need, and not gossiping about them. Love is about how we *treat* people, not how we *feel* about them.

I like for people to think about what they read in my books, so let me ask you some questions that will help you grow in love.

- Do you have any resentment in your heart?
- Are you ready to continue studying love and learning everything you can about it?
- Are you ready to humble yourself and be a peacemaker?
- How are you showing love to your enemies at this time in your life?
- In the past, how have you treated people in the past who are hard to love?
- How are you willing to treat them now?

If there is anything you realize you need to change in your life, ask God to help you. Study what His Word says about that topic so your mind will be renewed in that area. You will be tested, so don't be surprised when you are, but you can learn to pass your tests, and each one you pass makes you stronger.

The world is filled with increasing evil as each day goes by, but we can combat it with good. Be good to everyone and stay focused on love. Love God, love yourself by receiving God's love, and love other people. Let love flow out of you like a river. Appreciate people who help you and tell them you appreciate them. Compliment people, encourage them, smile, be friendly, and be very generous. Be helpful, kind, forgiving, and difficult to offend. In order for us to do these things, we need a lot of help from the Lord, so don't forget to lean on Him and ask for His grace frequently.

There will be times when we will fail, but we can repent and start fresh again. Love never fails, and it never gives up.

I'm so glad you read this book, and I hope you recommend it to other people. Love is what people in the world are looking for, even if they don't know it. A revival of God's love being poured out through His people will heal our broken world and empower us to leave a powerful, positive legacy to the next generation.

Love,

Joyce

SCRIPTURES TO HELP YOU FORGIVE AND FIND FREEDOM FROM OFFENSE

2 Chronicles 7:14

Psalm 32:5

Psalm 86:5

Psalm 103:10–14

Psalm 130:4

Proverbs 10:12

Proverbs 15:1

Proverbs 17:9

Proverbs 25:21

Proverbs 28:13

Isaiah 1:18

Isaiah 43:25–26

Isaiah 53:5

Isaiah 55:7

Jeremiah 31:34

Daniel 9:9

Micah 7:18–19

Zephaniah 3:17

Matthew 5:7

Matthew 5:23–24

Matthew 5:44

Matthew 6:12

Matthew 6:9–15

Matthew 18:15

Matthew 18:21–22

Matthew 26:28

Mark 11:25

Luke 6:27

Luke 6:37

Luke 17:3

John 13:34

Acts 3:19

Acts 10:43

Acts 13:38–39

Romans 8:1

Romans 12:17

Romans 12:20

1 Corinthians 13:5

Ephesians 1:7

Ephesians 4:31–32

Colossians 1:13–14

Colossians 3:13

Hebrews 8:12

James 2:8

James 5:16

1 Peter 3:9

1 Peter 4:8

1 John 1:9

1 John 2:1–2

Do you have a real relationship with Jesus?

God loves you! He created you to be a special, unique, one-of-a-kind individual, and He has a specific purpose and plan for your life. And through a personal relationship with your Creator—God—you can discover a way of life that will truly satisfy your soul.

No matter who you are, what you've done, or where you are in your life right now, God's love and grace are greater than your sin—your mistakes. Jesus willingly gave His life so you can receive forgiveness from God and have new life in Him. He's just waiting for you to invite Him to be your Savior and Lord.

If you are ready to commit your life to Jesus and follow Him, all you have to do is ask Him to forgive your sins and give you a fresh start in the life you are meant to live. Begin by praying this prayer...

Lord Jesus, thank You for giving Your life for me and forgiving me of my sins so I can have a personal relationship with You. I am sincerely sorry for the mistakes I've made, and I know I need You to help me live right.

Your Word says in Romans 10:9, "If you declare with your mouth, 'Jesus is Lord,' and believe in your heart that God raised him from the dead, you will be saved" (NIV). I believe You are the Son of God and confess You as my Savior and Lord. Take me just as I am, and work in my heart, making me the person You want me to be. I want to live for You, Jesus, and I am so grateful that You are giving me a fresh start in my new life with You today.

I love You, Jesus!

It's so amazing to know that God loves us so much! He wants to have a deep, intimate relationship with us that grows every day as we spend time with Him in prayer and Bible study. And we want to encourage you in your new life in Christ.

Please visit joycemeyer.org/salvation to request Joyce's book *A New Way of Living*, which is our gift to you. We also have other free resources online to help you make progress in pursuing everything God has for you.

Congratulations on your fresh start in your life in Christ! We hope to hear from you soon.

Joyce Meyer is one of the world's leading practical Bible teachers. A *New York Times* bestselling author, Joyce's books have helped millions of people find hope and restoration through Jesus Christ. Joyce's program *Enjoying Everyday Life* airs around the world on television, radio, and the internet. Through Joyce Meyer Ministries, Joyce teaches internationally on a number of topics with a particular focus on how the Word of God applies to our everyday lives. Her candid communication style allows her to share openly and practically about her experiences so others can apply what she has learned to their lives.

Joyce has authored more than 135 books, which have been translated into more than 160 languages, and over 37 million copies of her books have been distributed around the world free of charge. Bestsellers include *Power Thoughts*; *The Confident Woman*; *Look Great, Feel Great*; *Starting Your Day Right*; *Ending Your Day Right*; *Approval Addiction*; *How to Hear from God*; *Beauty for Ashes*; and *Battlefield of the Mind*.

Joyce's passion to help hurting people is foundational to the vision of Hand of Hope, the missions arm of Joyce Meyer Ministries. Hand of Hope provides worldwide humanitarian outreaches such as feeding programs, medical care, disaster response, human trafficking intervention and rehabilitation, and much more—always sharing the love and gospel of Christ.

Joyce Meyer Ministries—South Africa
P.O. Box 5
Cape Town 8000
South Africa
(27) 21-701-1056

Joyce Meyer Ministries—Francophonie
29 avenue Maurice Chevalier
77330 Ozoir la Ferriere
France

Joyce Meyer Ministries—Germany
Postfach 761001
22060 Hamburg
Germany
+49 (0)40 / 88 88 4 11 11

Joyce Meyer Ministries—Netherlands
Lorenzlaan 14
7002 HB Doetinchem
+31 657 555 9789

Joyce Meyer Ministries—Russia
P.O. Box 789
Moscow 101000
Russia
+7 (495) 727-14-68